A KID'S GUIDE TO BASEBALL LEGENDS

HOMERUNS, HISTORY AND INSPIRING STORIES FROM THE DIAMOND

KENT JAMESON

Published by:
Kent Jameson Publishing
kentjamesonpublishing@gmail.com
Printed in the United States of America.
First Printing, 2024
Library of Congress Cataloging-in-Publication Data:
Kent Jameson
A Kid's Guide To Baseball Legends: Homeruns, History and Inspiring Stories from the Diamond

TABLE OF CONTENTS

INTRODUCTION

When I was a kid, my summers had a rhythm all their own. The crack of the bat, the cheer of the crowd, and the smell of freshly cut grass were all part of the symphony. I remember our neighborhood baseball games, where everyone was a star in their own right. The dusty lot was our stadium, and every hit felt like a homerun.

Those moments sparked a passion in me that never faded. Baseball became more than a game. It became a lifelong love that I now want to share with you.

This book is here to inspire young readers like you. It's about bringing baseball to life with stories that captivate and excite. Whether you're a seasoned fan or new to the game, I want to make baseball as thrilling for you as it was for me. My goal is to make this book a bridge. A bridge that connects kids and families through the joys and lessons of baseball.

Baseball holds a special place in American culture. It has shaped our history and brought people together. From the founding of Major League Baseball to the unforgettable moments that have defined the sport, baseball is a thread that runs through the fabric of our nation. It's more than just a game. It's a shared experience that has united generations.

I wrote this book for parents, grandparents, and anyone who wants to share the magic of baseball with kids. It's designed to be a shared reading experience. One that brings families together through the stories of baseball's legendary players and teams. As you read, I hope you'll find moments to connect and share your own baseball memories.

Inside, you'll find chapters that take you on a journey through the history and heart of baseball. We'll explore legendary players who changed the game, modern icons who inspire new generations, and stories that show the true spirit of baseball. Each chapter has something special. It offers glimpses into the moments that make baseball so captivating.

I invite you to join me on this journey. As you turn the pages, you'll discover more than just facts and figures. You'll find stories that entertain, educate, and inspire. Baseball teaches us about teamwork, perseverance, and courage. These are lessons that go beyond the diamond.

Together, we'll explore the rich history of baseball and the inspiring stories that make it more than just a sport. So grab your glove, step up to the plate, and let's discover the magic of baseball together. The adventure awaits.

CHAPTER 1
THE ORIGINS OF
BASEBALL

1.1 FROM ROUNDERS TO BASEBALL: THE EARLY DAYS

I n England, rounders was a fun game for children. It involved a bat and a ball. Players aimed to hit the ball and run around bases to score. Sounds familiar, right? The game had its own set of rules. Players hit a ball with a bat, then ran around posts to score points. Unlike baseball, the pitcher bowled the ball underhand. Cricket also shared some parts with baseball. It involved hitting a ball and running to score. The main difference was that cricket had a wicket, not bases. It focused more on batting endurance and fielding strategy.

As these games reached America, people began to adjust and change them. Early Americans loved playing games in their free time. They started to mix elements from both rounders and cricket. This led to a new, unique game that we now know as baseball. Alexander Cartwright, a key figure, played a crucial role in this transition. In 1845, he helped create the Knickerbocker Rules, which laid the groundwork for modern baseball. These rules introduced the diamond-shaped field, the concept of three strikes, and even the idea of a foul ball.

Community games also played a major role in spreading baseball. Families would gather in fields or city parks. They would play informal games, enjoying the spirit of competition. These gatherings helped baseball grow from a pastime to a national passion. It became a game that brought people together, regardless of age or background. Urban settings saw kids playing in alleys or sandlots. In rural areas, fields became makeshift baseball diamonds. This widespread play helped baseball become a part of American life. It reflected values like teamwork, fairness, and community spirit.

As baseball started to gain popularity, some key figures emerged. They helped shape and guide the sport into what it is today. Abner Doubleday is often mentioned, though it's more myth than fact. Many believe he invented baseball in 1839, but historians doubt this tale. Instead, men like Henry Chadwick made real contributions. Chadwick, a sportswriter, introduced baseball statistics. He created the box score and batting average. These tools allowed fans to track player performance and compare teams. It added a layer of analysis to the game, making it more engaging.

The early days of baseball set the stage for what was to come. The game's growth mirrored the growth of America itself. It became a reflection of society, highlighting both its challenges and triumphs. Baseball's journey from informal play to organized sport is a testament to its enduring appeal. The game evolved, but it never lost its roots. It remained a simple yet profound way for people to connect. As you explore the history of baseball, remember that it is more than just a game. It is a story of innovation, tradition, and community.

1.2 THE BIRTH OF THE MAJOR LEAGUES: A NEW ERA BEGINS

The late 1800s marked a turning point for baseball. What began as informal games in parks and fields soon became something much bigger. The establishment of the Cincinnati Red Stockings in 1869 was a defining moment. They were the first professional baseball team, which meant they paid their players to play. This was a big change from the past when players played mainly for fun. The Red Stockings traveled widely, showcasing their talent and attracting fans with their thrilling, unbeaten season. This team showed that baseball could be more than just a pastime. It could become a profession. Following their success, more teams formed, and the idea of professional baseball began to take hold. In 1871, the National Association of Professional Base Ball Players was established. It was the first organized league where teams competed regularly. This structure allowed for consistent play and increased the sport's popularity.

The rise of professional baseball did not happen in a vacuum. The world around it was changing rapidly. America was in the midst of industrialization, which brought about new social and economic conditions. Factories and railroads transformed cities, providing both jobs and improved transportation. As people moved to urban areas for work, they found themselves with more leisure time. Baseball became a popular way to spend this free time. It was one of the earliest forms of mass entertainment. People from all walks of life gathered to watch games. It offered an escape from the daily grind, a chance to cheer, and a sense of community. The sport's growing popularity attracted investors and businessmen who saw potential profits. They started to organize teams and leagues, hoping to capitalize on the public's interest.

Creating these leagues was not without its challenges. Rivalries between teams quickly developed, sometimes leading to disputes and attempts to poach players from each other. Teams wanted the best talent, and this fierce competition could turn heated. Moreover, gambling emerged as a significant problem. Some players and even entire teams were accused of throwing games for money. This threatened the sport's reputation and raised concerns about its integrity. To address these issues, the National League was formed in 1876. It set strict rules to govern the sport, aiming to reduce corruption and stabilize the leagues. The introduction of the National League marked a new chapter for baseball, setting a standard for how professional leagues should operate.

The early days of major league baseball were filled with exciting developments. The first official season of the National League in 1876 was a key event. It laid the groundwork for organized play and consistency across teams. Another significant milestone was the introduction of the World Series. This annual event began in 1903 and brought together the best teams from the National and American Leagues. The World Series quickly became the highlight of the baseball season. It thrilled fans and crowned the ultimate champion. These events helped solidify baseball as America's favorite pastime. They set the stage for the sport's place in both culture and history.

1.3 EVOLUTION OF THE RULES: SHAPING THE GAME WE KNOW

The rules of baseball have changed a lot since the early days, making the game more exciting and fair. Imagine a time when pitchers tossed the ball underhand, like in a friendly backyard game. As baseball grew, so did the skills of its players. They started throwing overhand, adding speed and power to their pitches. This shift made hitting the ball much harder, changing how players approached their swings. With these changes, the game became more competitive. It pushed batters and pitchers to improve their tactics, keeping fans on the edge of their seats. Another important rule was the foul strike rule. Before this, foul balls didn't count as strikes. Batters could keep swinging without fear of striking out. By counting foul balls as strikes, the game sped up. This rule forced players to be more precise and strategic. It added a new layer of challenge, making each at-bat more thrilling.

Key figures played a crucial role in developing and refining baseball's rules. Henry Chadwick, often called the "Father of Baseball," introduced the scoring system. He created the box score, a way to record every detail of a game. This system allowed fans to follow the action even if they weren't there, making baseball more accessible to everyone. Albert Spalding also made a significant impact. He standardized baseball equipment, ensuring that every player used the same quality of gear. This level playing field meant that talent, not equipment, determined success. These contributions helped shape baseball into a more professional sport. Players could now focus on their skills, knowing that the rules and equipment were consistent.

Some rule changes sparked debate and controversy. The designated hitter rule, adopted by the American League in 1973, allowed teams to use a player to bat in place of the pitcher. This change aimed to boost offense and excitement. Fans loved seeing more hits and home runs, but purists argued it took away from the strategy of managing pitchers. On the other hand, some pitches faced bans due to safety concerns. The spitball, once a popular pitch, was banned in 1920. It gave pitchers an unfair grip advantage, making the ball unpredictable. This rule change focused on fairness and player safety. It showed how baseball adapted to protect its players while keeping the game competitive.

Baseball's rules continue to evolve in response to cultural and technological advancements. Instant replay, introduced in 2008, allows umpires to review close plays. This technology ensures accuracy, reducing errors in critical moments. It brings a modern touch to a traditional game, blending old with new. Safety concerns have also led to changes. Helmet mandates protect players from fast pitches. These rules show how baseball prioritizes player well-being. They reflect the sport's ongoing commitment to evolving with the times. Through these adjustments, baseball remains as dynamic as ever. It continues to capture the hearts of fans, offering timeless thrills and challenges.

1.4 ICONIC BASEBALL LOCATIONS: WHERE LEGENDS WERE MADE

Baseball has always been more than just a game. Its ballparks are not simply places where games are played. They are the homes of memories, where history is made and legends are born. Take Fenway Park, for example. Located in Boston, it's the oldest major-league stadium still in use. Fans know it for its Green Monster, a towering left-field wall that challenges hitters and excites fans. Fenway's quirky features and intimate setting create a unique atmosphere. It feels like stepping into a living museum, where every corner has a story to tell. Fenway is where the Boston Red Sox have built a legacy.

Then there's Wrigley Field in Chicago, with its ivy-covered outfield walls. This park is a gem of the Midwest, steeped in history and tradition. Wrigley is famous not only for its ivy but also its iconic hand-operated scoreboard. It is a classic baseball experience, where fans can watch games from bleachers on nearby rooftops. This setting offers a glimpse into the past. It reminds us of a time when baseball was the main event of summer days. Fans gather here to cheer on the Cubs, feeling part of something bigger than themselves.

Over the years, baseball stadiums have changed a lot. Early ballparks were simple wooden structures. They could not hold many people. As the sport grew, so did the need for bigger, more durable stadiums. Modern ballparks are made of steel and concrete. They can host thousands of fans. During the 1960s, multi-purpose stadiums became popular. These venues hosted baseball and other sports, like football. They were practical but often lacked the charm of older parks. Today, many teams aim to combine the best of both worlds. They create stadiums that offer modern amenities while keeping the nostalgic feel of classic ballparks.

Some of baseball's most memorable moments happened in these iconic locations. Babe Ruth's "called shot" at Wrigley Field in 1932 is one such event. Legend says Ruth pointed to the stands, then hit a home run where he pointed. It was an unforgettable moment that added to his larger-than-life persona. Similarly, Carlton Fisk's dramatic home run in Game 6 of the 1975 World Series is etched in baseball lore. At Fenway Park, Fisk waved his arms, hoping to keep the ball fair. It was a thrilling moment that captured the excitement and unpredictability of baseball.

These stadiums hold a special place in their communities. They become symbols of local pride and identity. Ebbets Field in Brooklyn once stood as a beloved landmark. It was more than a place for games. It was a gathering spot, a piece of Brooklyn's heart. Even today, people speak fondly of the Dodgers' years there. Yankee Stadium, known as "The House That Ruth Built," is another iconic venue. It represents the grandeur of New York City and its rich baseball history. Fans flock there, drawn by the aura of past triumphs and legendary players.

These ballparks, both past and present, serve as reminders of baseball's enduring appeal. They connect generations of fans, each bringing their own stories and memories. As you explore these historic locations, you feel part of something timeless. You walk the same paths as the greats who came before. The magic of these places lies not just in the games played, but in the sense of belonging they create. They are hallowed grounds where the spirit of baseball lives on.

CHAPTER 2

UNDERSTANDING
THE GAME

A sunny day, the smell of popcorn and hot dogs in the air, and the sound of a baseball hitting a glove. These are the moments that make baseball so special. But to truly enjoy the game, you need to understand its language. Baseball has its own set of words and phrases. These terms can seem like a secret code. But once you learn them, the game becomes even more exciting. Let's start with some of the key terms that every baseball fan should know.

One of the most exciting plays in baseball is the double play. It's a move that shows skill and teamwork. A batter hits the ball, and it rolls quickly towards the shortstop. The shortstop scoops it up and throws it to the second baseman. The second baseman catches it, steps on the base to get one runner out, and then throws it to the first baseman. The first baseman catches the ball just in time to get the batter out too. That's two outs in one play. It's a moment that can change the momentum of a game. A double play requires quick thinking and precise actions. It's one of those plays that gets fans on their feet, cheering for their team.

Another term that might puzzle you is the balk. This is a rule that keeps pitchers honest. When a pitcher is on the mound, they must follow certain rules. A balk happens when the pitcher starts their pitch but stops suddenly or makes an illegal move. This confuses the batter and runners. If a balk is called, any runners on base get to move forward one base. It's a rule that ensures fairness and prevents deception. Understanding a balk can help you appreciate the strategy behind pitching. It reminds us of the balance between offense and defense in baseball.

Now, let's talk about positions. The shortstop is one of the most crucial positions on the field. You can find the shortstop between second and third base. This player needs to have quick reflexes and strong arms. They often field ground balls and turn double plays. A good shortstop can make difficult plays look easy. Their role involves not only fielding but also communicating with other infielders to execute plays smoothly. The shortstop is a leader on the field, directing the defensive strategy and ensuring everyone is in the right position.

Catcher's interference is another term you might hear. This happens when the catcher accidentally hinders the batter's swing. If the batter makes contact with the catcher's glove while swinging, the umpire can call catcher's interference. This results in the batter being awarded first base. It's a rare play, but it highlights the delicate balance between offense and defense. The catcher must be close enough to catch the pitch but not so close that they interfere with the batter. It requires precision and awareness.

In baseball, strategy plays a big part. The sacrifice fly is a great example of this. When a batter hits a fly ball deep enough into the outfield, it allows a runner on third base to tag up and score after the catch. The batter gets out, but the team scores a run. This play shows the importance of teamwork and selflessness. The batter sacrifices their chance to get on base to help the team score.

Another strategic play is the hit and run. In this play, the runner on base starts running as soon as the pitcher throws the ball. The batter's job is to hit the ball into play, ideally into a gap in the field. This play can catch the defense off guard and advance runners into scoring positions. It requires precise timing and trust between the batter and runner.

Baseball has many unique expressions that add to its charm. Have you ever heard the term "around the horn"? This phrase describes the infielders' practice of throwing the ball around the bases after a strikeout with no runners on. It involves the third baseman, shortstop, second baseman, and first baseman tossing the ball in a circle. This helps keep their arms warm and is a tradition that adds flair to the game.

"Caught looking" is another phrase you might hear. This describes a batter who strikes out without swinging at the third strike. The batter stands frozen, watching the ball pass but unable to react. It's a moment that can be frustrating for the batter but thrilling for the pitcher and fans. It highlights the mental aspect of the game, where anticipation and quick decision-making are key.

Understanding these terms can enhance your enjoyment of baseball. They offer insights into the game's strategies and highlight the skills needed to succeed. Baseball is more than just a game of bat and ball. It's a dance of tactics and talent, where every player has a role to play. As you watch a game, try to spot these plays and terms in action. You'll find that they add depth and excitement to the experience.

2.1 FROM CAPS TO CLEATS: THE SIGNIFICANCE OF BASEBALL UNIFORMS

Imagine stepping onto a baseball field in the late 1800s. The players wear heavy, thick flannel uniforms that might seem more suited for cold weather. These early uniforms were made of wool and flannel, providing durability but little comfort in the summer heat. The first official baseball uniform was introduced in 1849 by the Knickerbocker Base Ball Club of New York City. It consisted of a white flannel shirt, blue wool pants, and a straw hat. Imagine playing under the sun in that outfit! Over time, uniforms have evolved significantly. Today, players wear uniforms made from synthetic blends. These materials are lighter, more breathable, and wick away sweat, allowing players to stay cool and comfortable during intense games. The evolution of baseball uniforms reflects the advancements in textile technology and the desire to enhance player performance.

Player numbers and team logos are now standard, but this wasn't always the case. The introduction of numbers on uniforms helped fans identify players more easily. Before this, fans had to rely on programs or announcements. Now, a quick glance tells you who's who. Team logos add another layer of identity. They connect fans with their favorite teams through symbols and colors. Think of the Yankees' iconic interlocking "NY" or the classic "B" on a Boston Red Sox cap. These symbols have become synonymous with their teams and evoke a sense of pride and belonging among fans. Logos are a vital part of the team's brand, appearing not just on uniforms but on merchandise and promotional materials.

Function plays a huge role in the design of baseball uniforms. Modern uniforms use breathable fabrics to keep players cool and dry. This comfort is crucial during long innings in the summer heat. Uniforms need to be flexible, allowing for a full range of motion. Players sprint, slide, and dive, so their clothing must move with them. Cleats, another key part of the uniform, provide traction and stability. Whether on grass or dirt, cleats help players maintain speed and balance. They are essential for quick starts, stops, and direction changes. Proper footwear can make a significant difference in a player's performance, reducing the risk of slipping and injury.

Uniforms also hold cultural significance. They foster team spirit and community identity. For instance, the Yankees' pinstripes are instantly recognizable. They've become a symbol of the team's storied history and success. Wearing the pinstripes links players to legends of the past. Uniforms create a sense of unity among team members. When players put on their jerseys, they become part of something bigger than themselves. They represent their team and community. The colors and designs of uniforms can evoke strong emotions and memories among fans, creating a lasting connection between the team and its supporters.

Caps hold a special place in baseball culture. They serve a practical purpose by shielding players' eyes from the sun. This allows them to track high fly balls and focus on the game. But caps are more than just functional. They are a cultural fashion statement. Fans wear them to show their support for their favorite team. Over time, baseball caps have become a staple in casual fashion. They've transcended the sport, appearing in various styles and colors. The cap's simple yet iconic design makes it versatile and widely recognized. Wearing a baseball cap can be a way to express personal style while also signaling allegiance to a particular team.

The transformation of baseball uniforms from heavy wool to sleek modern designs mirrors the broader changes in the sport. As baseball evolved, so did the attire, adapting to meet the needs of the players and fans. The uniform is more than just clothing. It is a symbol of tradition, identity, and the ever-changing landscape of baseball. Whether it's the classic look of the Yankees or the vibrant colors of newer teams, each uniform tells a story. It connects the past with the present, linking generations of players and fans in the shared experience of America's pastime.

2.2 THE TOOLS OF THE TRADE: ESSENTIAL BASEBALL EQUIPMENT

In the game of baseball, each player takes the field with a unique set of tools. These items are more than just gear; they are extensions of the player. A glove, for instance, is essential. It comes in different shapes and sizes, each tailored to a specific position. Outfielders use larger gloves to catch fly balls, while infielders prefer smaller ones for quick throws. Catchers have mitts with extra padding to handle fast pitches. First basemen use gloves with a curved edge to scoop up low throws. Each type serves a purpose, helping players perform their best.

The bat is another critical piece of equipment. Traditionally made of wood, bats now also come in aluminum and composite materials. Wooden bats, often made from ash or maple, provide a solid feel and sound. They are the standard in professional leagues. Aluminum bats are lighter and used in amateur play, offering greater swing speed and distance. Composite bats combine materials, enhancing durability and performance. The choice of bat can affect a player's swing, control, and confidence. It's not just about hitting the ball; it's about the right feel in the hands.

Many players customize their equipment to fit their needs. A well-fitted glove is crucial for comfort and grip. Players often use oils and conditioners to break in new gloves, making them flexible and easier to use. This process creates a glove that feels like an extension of the hand. Batting gloves are worn for better grip and to protect hands from blisters. They provide an extra layer between the bat and the skin, enhancing control during the swing. Personalization helps players feel secure and focused, knowing their gear suits them perfectly.

Advancements in technology have greatly improved baseball equipment. Helmets now feature enhanced protection, using materials that absorb impact better. They safeguard players against high-speed pitches. Catcher's gear has also evolved. Modern chest protectors and masks are lighter yet more protective. This allows catchers to move swiftly while staying safe. These advancements reflect a commitment to player safety, enabling athletes to play with confidence. The improvements in gear have reduced injuries, allowing players to focus more on the game and less on potential harm.

Rituals and superstitions often accompany the use of equipment. Many players have pre-game rituals involving their gear. They might tap their bat against the plate a certain number of times or adjust their gloves before each pitch. These routines help players focus and feel mentally prepared. Some believe certain bats bring good luck, using them only in crucial situations. Others might have lucky socks or a favorite cap that they wear for every game. These rituals are part of the mental game, providing comfort and a sense of control.

Baseball is rich with traditions that extend to its equipment. The tools of the game are not just physical objects; they hold sentimental value. They are part of a player's identity, shaping how they approach each inning. From the crack of the bat to the snap of a glove, these elements create the symphony that is baseball. By understanding the equipment, we gain insight into the player's world. It's a reminder that even in a game as old as baseball, there is always room for innovation and personal touch. These tools connect players to the history of the game, while also paving the way for the future.

2.3 BASEBALL SLANG DECODED: SPEAKING LIKE A PRO

Baseball has its own language. This language makes the game unique and fun. When you're at a game, you might hear someone shout, "He hit a dinger!" A dinger is a home run. It's a big hit that sends the ball over the fence, allowing the batter to circle all the bases. Hearing this word fills the park with excitement. Everyone knows it's a moment worth cheering. Then there's "southpaw," which refers to a left-handed pitcher. The term comes from how baseball fields used to be laid out. With the batter facing east, a left-handed pitcher's throwing arm pointed south. Both terms show how baseball's language is rooted in its history and play.

Some terms describe the action on the field. A "frozen rope" is a line drive. It's a ball hit hard and fast, traveling in a straight line across the field. This kind of hit is tough for fielders to catch. It often results in a base hit. Players and fans love seeing a frozen rope because it shows the batter's power and precision. On the other hand, a "golden sombrero" isn't as celebrated. It refers to a player who strikes out four times in a single game. While not a proud moment, it's a part of the game, reminding players that even the best have tough days.

Slang adds to the fun of baseball. It brings players and fans together. Players use playful terms during games to lighten the mood. They might call a teammate "ace" for a good pitch or "slugger" for a powerful hit. This banter builds camaraderie, making the team feel like a family. Fans join in, adopting these terms and shouting them from the stands. This shared language connects everyone and creates a lively atmosphere.

Baseball slang can vary by region. On the West Coast, you might hear "can of corn" for an easy catch, while the East Coast might call it a "pop fly." These differences add flavor to the game. They show how baseball reflects the diverse culture of its fans. Even leagues have their own slang. In the American League, you might hear about a "designated hitter," while the National League discusses "pitchers hitting." This variety enriches the sport, making each game unique.

Understanding baseball slang can make watching the game more fun. It helps you feel like part of the community, whether you're at the ballpark or watching from home. Each term tells a story, carrying with it the spirit of the game. As you learn these words, you'll find yourself speaking like a pro, sharing in the excitement and tradition of baseball with everyone around you.

Slang is just one part of the bigger picture. It shows how language can bring people together. As we move forward, we'll dive deeper into the stories of the legends and heroes that make baseball unforgettable. Let's continue to explore the magic of this great game.

CHAPTER 3
LEGENDS OF THE PAST

3.1 BABE RUTH: THE SULTAN OF SWAT

Baseball has always been a game full of heroes. One name that stands out is Babe Ruth, often called "The Sultan of Swat." Imagine the early days of baseball, where strategy leaned towards small ball. Teams focused on bunting, stealing bases, and getting singles. Then came Babe Ruth, who changed the game forever. He saw the potential in power hitting. With every swing, he aimed for the fences. He made home runs more than just a rare event. They became a thrilling part of the game. People came to the ballpark hoping to see Ruth hit one out of the park. His ability to set home run records captured the imagination of fans everywhere. It wasn't just about the numbers he put up. It was about the excitement and energy he brought to the field.

Babe Ruth wasn't just a great player. He was a larger-than-life figure who drew people to baseball. His charisma and charm made him a favorite among fans and the media. He had a knack for drawing attention, both for his skills and his personality. Ruth had a way of making headlines. He was often photographed and talked about, becoming a household name. This media presence helped boost baseball's popularity during its golden age. People who had never watched a game before became fans because of Ruth. He became a cultural icon, representing not just baseball but the spirit of the 1920s. His presence on and off the field helped baseball grow into America's pastime.

One of the most famous moments in Babe Ruth's career happened during the 1932 World Series. The New York Yankees were playing against the Chicago Cubs at Wrigley Field. According to legend, during the fifth inning, Ruth pointed to center field before hitting a home run to that exact spot. This moment became known as "The Called Shot." While some argue about whether he really called it, the story remains a part of baseball folklore. This game also showed Ruth's ability to perform under pressure. His transition from a pitcher to an outfielder further showcased his versatility. As a pitcher, Ruth had already made a name for himself with the Boston Red Sox. By moving to the outfield, he could focus on hitting and became even more of a star.

Ruth's impact went beyond his playing days. He influenced future generations of baseball players. Many sluggers who came after him looked to Ruth as a model. They tried to emulate his powerful swing and fearless approach. Ruth's style of play paved the way for modern power hitters. Players like Hank Aaron and Barry Bonds built on the foundation Ruth laid. He showed that baseball could be both strategic and exciting. His influence also extended to the business side of baseball. Ruth's popularity helped commercialize the sport. His endorsements and appearances showed that athletes could be stars beyond the diamond. This commercialization opened up new opportunities for players.

Babe Ruth's legacy is a testament to the power of sports to inspire and transform. His larger-than-life persona and game-changing skills made him a legend. Baseball, as we know it today, owes much to Ruth's contributions. He set the stage for a more dynamic and thrilling game. His story is a reminder of how one person's passion and talent can leave a lasting mark on history.

Reflection Section: Babe Ruth's Influence

Think about Babe Ruth's impact on baseball. How did his style of play change the game? Can you see his influence in the way modern players approach hitting? Take a moment to reflect on how one player can shape an entire sport.

3.2 JACKIE ROBINSON: BREAKING BARRIERS

Jackie Robinson's entry into Major League Baseball was nothing short of groundbreaking. It was 1947 when he signed with the Brooklyn Dodgers, becoming the first African American to play in the major leagues during the modern era. This was a time when racial segregation was still the norm in many parts of America.

Robinson's presence on the field challenged those norms and opened doors for countless others. His debut wasn't just a baseball moment. It was a pivotal event in American history. By stepping onto the field, Robinson took a stand against the segregation that had kept black players out of Major League Baseball. His courage and determination changed the game forever.

Robinson faced immense challenges, both on and off the field. Many fans and players were hostile towards him. They hurled insults and threats, trying to shake his resolve. But Robinson remained composed. He met each challenge with dignity and strength. His resilience under such pressure was remarkable. He knew he was not just playing for himself. He was playing for future generations. Robinson's ability to maintain his poise in the face of adversity made him a hero. He showed the world that talent and character mattered more than skin color. His bravery inspired others to stand up against injustice and fight for equality.

On the field, Robinson's performance spoke volumes. In his first year, he won the Rookie of the Year Award, showcasing his incredible talent. He had a powerful combination of speed, skill, and intelligence. This made him a standout player. He stole bases with ease and hit with precision, contributing to his team's success. But Robinson's impact went beyond baseball. He used his platform to advocate for racial equality. He spoke out against discrimination and worked tirelessly to promote civil rights. His activism helped push for change in both sports and society. Robinson's efforts laid the groundwork for future progress, inspiring others to use their voices for good.

Robinson's legacy endures today, continuing to inspire new generations. Every year on April 15, Major League Baseball celebrates Jackie Robinson Day. On this day, players across the league wear his number, 42, in his honor. This tradition reminds us of Robinson's courage and the barriers he broke down. His story is more than a tale of athletic achievement. It's a powerful narrative of courage and equality. Robinson became a symbol of the fight for justice, showing what one person can achieve with determination and effort. His influence extends beyond sports, resonating in the broader struggle for civil rights and equality.

Robinson's life and career are testaments to the power of perseverance. He showed that one person can change the world. His story continues to inspire athletes, activists, and everyday people. Through his actions, Robinson taught us that standing up for what's right is always worth the struggle. His legacy is a beacon of hope. It encourages us to strive for a fairer, better world. Robinson's impact is felt every time a player of color steps onto a major league field. His courage paved the way for a more inclusive future, breaking barriers that once seemed insurmountable.

3.3 LOU GEHRIG: THE IRON HORSE'S LEGACY

Lou Gehrig, known as "The Iron Horse," set a standard in baseball that few have matched. His career was marked by an incredible streak of playing in 2,130 consecutive games. This record stood for decades, showcasing not only his talent but also his resilience. Gehrig was a powerhouse on the field. He consistently delivered high performance, earning two MVP awards and numerous All-Star selections. His batting average and home runs were among the best in the league. But beyond the numbers, it was his unwavering dedication that left a lasting impression. Gehrig played through injuries and tough conditions, demonstrating a level of endurance that made him a role model for athletes everywhere.

Gehrig's sportsmanship and character were as notable as his athletic achievements. He was known for his humility, always putting the team first. On and off the field, Gehrig conducted himself with grace and respect. He was well-liked by teammates and fans alike, earning admiration for his quiet strength and integrity. Gehrig never sought the spotlight, yet it found him because of his exemplary conduct. His relationships with others in the sport were built on mutual respect. Fans saw him as approachable and genuine, a player who played for the love of the game. This reputation made him one of the most beloved figures in baseball history.

The end of Gehrig's career was both poignant and impactful. In 1939, he was diagnosed with amyotrophic lateral sclerosis (ALS), a disease that would later bear his name. Forced to retire, Gehrig addressed fans with his famous "Luckiest Man" speech at Yankee Stadium. He spoke with gratitude despite his challenges, calling himself lucky for having had the support of his family, friends, and fans. This speech moved everyone present and has become one of the most memorable moments in sports history. Gehrig's retirement brought attention to ALS, raising awareness and prompting research into the disease. His courage in the face of illness inspired many, showing that true strength lies in one's character and spirit.

Gehrig's legacy continues to influence future generations. He remains a symbol of perseverance and determination, embodying the qualities that athletes strive for. His story inspires not only those in sports but also those facing their challenges. Gehrig's impact on sports medicine and ALS research is significant. His case highlighted the need for better understanding and treatment of the disease. Today, his name is synonymous with the fight against ALS, encouraging efforts to find a cure. Athletes look to Gehrig as a model of how to handle adversity with dignity and grace.

Gehrig's life and career are reminders of what it means to be a true sportsman. His achievements on the field were matched by his character off it, setting a benchmark for all who follow. The Iron Horse's legacy is one of resilience, humility, and inspiration.

3.4 HONUS WAGNER: THE FLYING DUTCHMAN

Honus Wagner's story begins long before the bright lights of Major League Baseball. Born to humble beginnings, Wagner started life in a coal-mining town in Pennsylvania. His early years were spent working in the mines, a tough and grueling environment. But even then, his love for baseball was evident. It was the game that offered him a glimpse of something more, a way out of the coal dust. His talent on the field soon became undeniable. He began playing for local teams, his skills catching the eyes of scouts. Wagner's journey to the majors began with the Louisville Colonels, where he quickly made a name for himself. His success there paved the way for his legendary career with the Pittsburgh Pirates.

Known for his versatility, Wagner excelled in multiple positions. While he is most famous as a shortstop, his abilities extended across the field. His adaptability made him a valuable player, one who could fill any gap as needed. This versatility helped him lead the Pittsburgh Pirates to great success. As a shortstop, he set the standard for future players. His fielding was sharp, and his base running was precise. Wagner's strategic mind made him a leader on the field, guiding his team with a calm and steady hand. His contributions to the Pirates were immense, helping them win multiple pennants and solidifying their place in baseball history.

Wagner's influence on baseball went beyond his playing skills. He was a thinker, always looking for ways to improve the game. His innovations in base running and fielding techniques changed how the sport was played. Wagner's keen understanding of the game's mechanics allowed him to outthink his opponents. His approach to playing shortstop revolutionized the position. He showed that it was not just about catching balls but also about strategy and intelligence. Wagner's influence is still felt today, as modern shortstops continue to follow in his footsteps. His legacy as a strategic innovator remains an integral part of baseball's evolution.

One of Wagner's most enduring legacies is his famous baseball card. The T206 Honus Wagner card is one of the rarest and most valuable in the world. Its rarity stems from Wagner's own refusal to have it produced in large numbers. Some say he objected to promoting tobacco to children, while others suggest he was unhappy with the compensation. Whatever the reason, this decision has made the card a sought-after piece of memorabilia. Its value has soared over the years, selling for millions at auctions. This card is more than just a collector's item. It symbolizes Wagner's unique place in baseball history. His impact on the sport was so profound that a small piece of cardboard bearing his image became a treasure.

Wagner's contributions to baseball were recognized when he was inducted into the Baseball Hall of Fame. He was among the first group of players honored, a testament to his influence and achievements. His legacy continues to inspire players and fans alike. Wagner's life is a story of hard work, talent, and vision. He showed that with determination, anyone could rise from humble beginnings to achieve greatness. His impact on baseball is still felt today, as players strive to match his skill and dedication. Wagner's story is a reminder of how the game can change lives and leave a lasting legacy.

CHAPTER 4
MODERN DAY ICONS

4.1 DEREK JETER: THE CAPTAIN'S JOURNEY

When you think of baseball heroes today, Derek Jeter's name often comes up. He grew up in Michigan with big dreams and a fierce love for baseball. His journey from a hopeful child to the team's captain is a story of dedication and skill. Jeter played twenty memorable years with the New York Yankees. He became a symbol of leadership and excellence. Let's explore what made him such a remarkable player and how his impact extends beyond the baseball field.

As the captain of the Yankees, Jeter led with a quiet strength that inspired his teammates. He wasn't just about words; he let his actions speak for themselves. Jeter's leadership showed in the way he played the game. He contributed to five World Series championships, being the heart and soul of the team. Fans remember him for his clutch performances in the postseason. He earned the nickname "Captain Clutch" for his ability to deliver when it mattered most. Jeter's presence on the field was calming and powerful. His teammates knew they could count on him, whether it was making a big play or hitting a crucial home run. His leadership helped the Yankees maintain their tradition of excellence.

Jeter's consistency is one of his defining traits. Over his career, he amassed more than 3,000 hits, a milestone few players reach. Each hit was a testament to his skill and determination. Jeter's ability to perform at such a high level year after year set him apart. He won five Gold Glove Awards for his outstanding defense. He also received five Silver Slugger Awards for his hitting. These awards show his all-around excellence as a player. Jeter's work ethic was legendary. He trained hard and stayed focused, always striving to improve. His dedication inspired young players to follow his example, emphasizing the importance of persistence and hard work.

Off the field, Jeter's influence is just as significant. He founded the Turn 2 Foundation, aiming to help young people avoid drugs and alcohol. The foundation promotes healthy living and positive choices. Through his efforts, Jeter has inspired countless young people to make better decisions. He emphasized education and community involvement, encouraging kids to aim high. Jeter also served as a mentor to younger players, sharing his knowledge and experiences. He became an ambassador for baseball, representing the sport with dignity and respect. His off-field contributions highlight his commitment to making a difference in the world.

Jeter's career had a cultural impact that goes beyond baseball. He became a global sports icon, known for his sportsmanship and success. His approach to the game and life earned him respect worldwide. Young athletes look up to him as a role model. Jeter showed them that success comes from hard work, integrity, and perseverance. His influence extends to future generations of players. They strive to emulate his dedication and character. In a world where athletes often make headlines for the wrong reasons, Jeter stood out as someone who used his platform for good. He showed that being a great athlete also means being a great person. His legacy continues to inspire those who dream of greatness.

Reflection Section: What Makes a Leader?

Think about what makes someone a leader. Is it their actions, their words, or both? Reflect on how Derek Jeter led his team and inspired others. Consider how you can apply similar principles in your own life, whether in sports, school, or at home.

4.2 ALBERT PUJOLS: POWER AND PRECISION

Albert Pujols is a name that echoes through the halls of baseball greatness. With over 600 career home runs, his power at the plate is legendary. Pujols isn't just about strength; he combines it with precision. His ability to hit the ball with force and accuracy makes him one of the most feared batters in the game. Winning the National League MVP award three times shows his dominance.

Each season, he delivered performances that left fans in awe. Pujols's swing is a marvel, a blend of raw power and refined technique. He studied opposing pitchers, learning their habits and anticipating their moves. This preparation gave him an edge, allowing him to adjust his approach and deliver when needed. His discipline at the plate was unmatched. He maintained consistent mechanics, ensuring that his swing was always ready to connect. Pujols's attention to detail and focus on preparation set him apart from others.

Pujols's impact on his teams was immense. He played a key role in the St. Louis Cardinals' success, leading them to multiple World Series victories. His leadership in the clubhouse was vital. Younger players looked up to him, learning from his work ethic and dedication. Pujols was more than a star player; he was a mentor and a guide. His presence on the team lifted everyone around him, creating an environment where talent could thrive. He understood the importance of teamwork and led by example, showing that true success is built on collaboration and shared goals.

Off the field, Pujols's contributions are just as impressive. He founded the Pujols Family Foundation, focusing on supporting individuals with Down syndrome. The foundation provides resources and opportunities, helping families navigate the challenges they face. Pujols's commitment to this cause is personal and heartfelt, driven by his love for his own child with Down syndrome. His work extends to the Dominican Republic, where he has given back to his homeland. Through various initiatives, Pujols has improved lives and provided hope. Whether building homes or supporting education, his impact is far-reaching. He used his platform to make a difference, showing that being a great athlete also means being a great human.

Pujols's career and legacy are built on a foundation of power, precision, and compassion. His achievements on the field are matched by his contributions off it. He has inspired countless fans and players, showing them what's possible with hard work and dedication. Pujols's story is one of triumph, both in sports and in life. His influence continues to resonate, leaving a mark that will be felt for generations.

4.3 ICHIRO SUZUKI: A GLOBAL SENSATION

Imagine stepping into a new world, where everything is different. That's what Ichiro Suzuki did when he joined Major League Baseball from Japan. He paved the way as the first Japanese-born position player to play in MLB. When Ichiro debuted with the Seattle Mariners in 2001, he brought with him a unique style that left fans and players alike in awe. His rookie season was nothing short of spectacular. He not only won the Rookie of the Year but also the MVP award. These accomplishments set the tone for a career that would see him collect over 3,000 hits. Each hit was a testament to his skill and perseverance. Ichiro's success wasn't just about numbers. It was about breaking barriers and setting new standards. His transition to MLB was seamless, and he showed that talent knows no borders.

Ichiro's playing style was unlike anything seen before. He focused on speed and contact hitting, which was a departure from the power hitting that many MLB players favored. His quick feet allowed him to steal bases and cover ground in the outfield with ease. Ichiro's defensive skills were just as impressive as his batting. He had a strong arm that made runners think twice before trying to advance on him. This combination of speed and precision made Ichiro a standout player. His ability to make contact with almost any pitch baffled pitchers and delighted fans. Ichiro's approach to the game was both strategic and artistic. He didn't just play baseball; he made it a spectacle. His style challenged the conventions of the sport and showed that there was more than one way to succeed.

Ichiro's impact went beyond the field. He became a bridge between cultures, bringing Japan and America closer through baseball. His success in MLB opened doors for other Japanese players, inspiring them to pursue their dreams in the major leagues. Ichiro was more than a player; he was a symbol of hope and possibility for many. His global fanbase grew rapidly, drawing attention from all corners of the world. People admired his dedication and the way he respected the sport. Ichiro's presence in MLB helped increase the game's popularity in Japan, making it a truly international sport. His story demonstrated that baseball was not just an American pastime; it was a game that could unite people from different backgrounds and cultures.

Ichiro's legacy in baseball is profound. He changed how people viewed international players and inspired a new generation of athletes. Both in Japan and the U.S., he is celebrated as a trailblazer who showed that hard work and passion could overcome any obstacle. Ichiro's influence on the globalization of baseball talent is undeniable. He proved that the sport could be enriched by diverse playing styles and cultural influences. His career is a shining example of how sports can break down barriers and bring people together. Ichiro's journey continues to inspire those who dream of making their mark on the world stage. His story is a testament to the power of perseverance and the universal language of baseball.

4.4 CLAYTON KERSHAW: MASTER OF THE MOUND

Clayton Kershaw stands tall among baseball's greatest pitchers. His career with the Los Angeles Dodgers is filled with impressive achievements. Kershaw has won multiple Cy Young Awards, which honor the best pitchers in the league. He also earned the MVP award, showing his all-around dominance. His career statistics speak for themselves. He consistently maintains a low ERA, which measures how few runs he allows per game. This shows his skill in keeping opponents from scoring. Kershaw's ability to strike out batters is another testament to his talent. He's known for sending hitters back to the bench, unable to connect with his pitches. These achievements place him among the best in baseball history.

Kershaw's success on the mound comes from more than just natural talent. His pitching techniques are a big part of his dominance. He uses a combination of a fastball and a curveball that keeps batters guessing. The fastball comes in fast and straight, challenging hitters to react quickly. His curveball, on the other hand, drops suddenly, making it hard for batters to make solid contact. This mix of speed and deception is a key part of his success. Kershaw's mental approach is just as important. He prepares rigorously for each game, studying opponents and planning his pitches. His training regimen is intense, focusing on both physical and mental strength. This preparation allows him to execute his game plan with precision, leaving little room for error.

Kershaw is not just a great pitcher; he's also a leader for the Dodgers. His influence extends beyond his performances on the field. He played a key role in ending the Dodgers' long World Series drought, helping them win the championship. His leadership inspires confidence in his teammates. Younger pitchers look up to him, learning from his experience and work ethic. Kershaw mentors them, helping them develop their skills and find their place on the team. He leads by example, showing that hard work and dedication pay off. His presence in the clubhouse is steady and calming, helping the team stay focused on their goals.

Off the field, Kershaw is known for his generosity and kindness. He started Kershaw's Challenge, a charity that supports communities in need. This initiative shows his commitment to making a difference beyond baseball. The charity focuses on building and supporting projects that help children and families. Kershaw's involvement in these efforts highlights his character. He's known as a humble and charitable athlete, someone who uses his success to help others. His reputation as a good person is as strong as his reputation as a pitcher. Through his philanthropic work, Kershaw shows that being a great athlete means giving back to the community.

Clayton Kershaw's story is one of talent, hard work, and heart. His achievements on the mound are matched by his contributions off it. He inspires not just his teammates, but fans around the world. His legacy in baseball is secure, as he continues to build on his successes. Kershaw's influence reaches far beyond the Dodgers, impacting the sport and community. As we move forward, his example reminds us of the power of dedication and giving back.

As we wrap up our look at modern baseball icons, we see how each player leaves a unique mark on the game. From hitting and fielding to pitching, they shape baseball's future. Next, we'll step into the world of home run legends, where the power of the swing takes center stage.

CHAPTER 5
HOMERUN HEROES

Home runs are more than just points on the scoreboard. They are symbols of skill, power, and determination. In this chapter, we explore the stories of those who have become legends through their ability to hit the ball out of the park. These players have captured the hearts of fans and left a lasting impact on the game. Let's begin with Hank Aaron, a name synonymous with grace and greatness.

5.1 HANK AARON: A RECORD-BREAKING CAREER

Hank Aaron's journey to becoming the home run king is a tale of perseverance and resilience. He grew up in a time when racial prejudice was a harsh reality. Despite the challenges, Aaron never let that stop him. He faced discrimination and adversity head-on, using them as fuel to drive his success. His dedication to the game and his work ethic set him apart. Aaron's consistent performance on the field eventually led him to surpass Babe Ruth's home run record, a feat many thought impossible. On April 8, 1974, in front of a sellout crowd at Atlanta-Fulton County Stadium, Aaron hit his 715th home run off Al Downing of the Dodgers. This monumental achievement not only broke the record but also shattered racial barriers, proving that talent knows no bounds.

Aaron's contributions to baseball extend far beyond his home run record. He was a complete player, excelling in all aspects of the game. Over his career, Aaron achieved remarkable stats, with a total of 755 home runs, 2,297 RBIs, and 6,856 total bases, records that still stand today. His ability to hit for both power and average made him a force to be reckoned with. Aaron's influence as an all-around player inspired countless others to strive for excellence. He showed that success in baseball requires more than just strength. It needs intelligence, strategy, and dedication.

In the broader context of American society, Aaron's achievement was profound. During the Civil Rights Movement, his record-breaking moment served as a beacon of hope and progress. It reminded the nation of the power of determination and dignity in the face of adversity. Aaron's career broke down barriers and opened doors for future generations of athletes. He became a symbol of perseverance, showing that hard work and integrity can overcome even the toughest obstacles. His story resonated far beyond the baseball diamond, becoming an integral part of the fight for equality.

Aaron's legacy continues to inspire, long after his retirement. The Hank Aaron Award, given to the best offensive player in each league, honors his contributions to the sport. Through this award, Aaron's influence endures, encouraging players to aim for greatness. His impact on diversity and inclusion in sports is significant. Aaron paved the way for players of all backgrounds to pursue their dreams. His story remains a source of motivation for young athletes, teaching them the value of resilience and hard work. Aaron's life and career are testaments to the idea that with determination and strength, anything is possible.

Reflection Section: Hank Aaron's Impact

Think about the challenges Hank Aaron faced and how he overcame them. Consider how his story of perseverance and success can inspire you or the young athletes in your life. What lessons can you take from Aaron's journey and apply to your own path, whether in sports, school, or everyday life?

5.2 BARRY BONDS: CONTROVERSIES AND TRIUMPHS

Barry Bonds is a name that stirs debate among baseball fans. His journey to become the all-time home run leader is filled with both glory and controversy. Bonds hit an astonishing 762 home runs, surpassing Hank Aaron's long-standing record. This achievement came after years of hard work and talent on the field. Bonds had a natural ability that few could match. But his career was not without its shadows. Allegations of performance-enhancing drug use cast a long shadow over his accomplishments. Many questioned if those substances played a role in his home run record. This controversy has affected how people remember his career. Some view him as a great talent, while others see him as a symbol of a troubled era in baseball.

Bonds was known for his exceptional approach to hitting. He had remarkable plate discipline. This means he knew when to swing and when to let the ball go. He rarely struck out and had a keen eye for pitches outside the strike zone. This skill helped him achieve a high on-base percentage, meaning he reached base frequently, whether by hits or walks. Bonds also had a powerful swing, which helped him hit many home runs. His mechanics were precise, allowing him to connect with the ball with great force. He studied pitchers carefully, learning their habits and weaknesses. This strategic mindset made him a formidable opponent. His ability to anticipate and react to pitches was unmatched, making him a constant threat at the plate.

The duality of Bonds's legacy is a subject of much discussion. On one hand, his records and accolades are impressive. He won seven MVP awards and set numerous hitting records. These achievements show his talent and impact on the game. On the other hand, public perception is shaped by the controversies surrounding him. The allegations of steroid use have led to debates about his place in baseball history. Bonds has not been inducted into the Hall of Fame, despite his accomplishments. This exclusion has sparked discussions about what criteria should be used to judge a player's legacy. Some argue that his on-field achievements should be enough, while others believe the allegations cannot be ignored.

Bonds's career has broader implications for baseball. It has influenced discussions about ethics and the role of performance-enhancing drugs in sports. His story has been used as a case study in how talent and controversy can coexist. Bonds's situation has prompted baseball to take a closer look at its policies and practices. The debates about his legacy continue to impact how the sport is viewed. They have led to increased scrutiny and changes in how players are evaluated. Bonds's story highlights the complexities of balancing individual achievements with the integrity of the game. His impact on baseball will be felt for years to come, as the sport continues to grapple with these issues.

5.3 MARK MCGWIRE: THE SUMMER OF '98

In the summer of 1998, baseball fans found themselves on the edge of their seats. Mark McGwire, playing for the St. Louis Cardinals, was chasing a record that many thought would stand forever. The single-season home run record set by Roger Maris in 1961 was a big milestone. McGwire, with his powerful swing, was on track to break it. What made this chase even more exciting was his rivalry with Sammy Sosa of the Chicago Cubs. Both players were hitting home runs at a pace that had fans buzzing. The competition was friendly but fierce, capturing the attention of the entire nation. Every game turned into a must-watch event. People wanted to see if one of them would hit another home run and how close they were getting to the record. McGwire eventually hit his 62nd home run on September 8, surpassing Maris. He finished the season with an astonishing 70 home runs. This feat reignited interest in baseball, especially after the strike in 1994 left many fans disheartened.

McGwire's ability to hit so many home runs didn't come by luck. It was a result of dedication and hard work. He focused heavily on strength training, using weights to build the muscle needed to drive the ball over the fences. This focus on strength gave him the power needed to hit home runs consistently. His batting stance was another key to his success. Over the years, McGwire adjusted his stance to improve his balance and timing. He kept his feet wide and his knees slightly bent, giving him a solid base. This base allowed him to generate power from his legs, which transferred up through his swing. His approach to hitting was methodical, always looking to improve and refine his technique. By studying pitchers and understanding their tendencies, McGwire could anticipate pitches and time his swings perfectly. This combination of strength and strategy made him one of the most feared hitters in the league.

After McGwire's incredible season, the baseball world learned more about what fueled those home runs. McGwire admitted to using performance-enhancing drugs during his career. This revelation changed how people viewed his achievements. The use of steroids was a part of what became known as baseball's steroid era. This era raised questions about fairness and the integrity of the game. Fans and players alike began to wonder how many records were genuine and how many were tainted. McGwire's admission was a turning point. It led to stricter drug testing and policies in MLB. The league worked hard to regain trust and ensure a level playing field. The discussions about steroids continue to this day, with McGwire's story often at the center of those conversations. It sparked an ongoing dialogue about ethics in sports and what it means to compete fairly.

Despite the controversies, McGwire found a way to remain connected to baseball. He transitioned into coaching, sharing his knowledge with the next generation of players. As a mentor, he focused on teaching young athletes about hitting and the importance of playing the game the right way. His experience as a player offered valuable insights into the challenges and pressures of professional baseball. McGwire's influence on younger players is significant. He encouraged them to focus on skill and strategy, emphasizing the importance of hard work and dedication. His role as a coach allowed him to give back to the sport, helping shape future stars and contributing to baseball's ongoing legacy.

5.4 SAMMY SOSA: A POWER HITTER'S JOURNEY

Sammy Sosa's story in baseball is one of resilience, power, and a bit of flair. Born in the Dominican Republic, Sosa grew up dreaming of playing in the big leagues. His journey to stardom began with the Texas Rangers at a young age, but it was with the Chicago Cubs that Sosa truly found his place. As a Cub, his power at the plate became legendary. Fans flocked to see him hit towering home runs that seemed to defy gravity. His breakout year came in 1998 when he found himself in a historic home run race against Mark McGwire. That summer, Sosa and McGwire chased Roger Maris's single-season home run record, captivating fans across the nation. Sosa finished with 66 home runs, earning the National League MVP award and forever cementing his place in baseball history. His ability to hit home runs with such consistency led him to the 600-home run milestone, a rare feat that only a few players have achieved.

Sosa's impact on baseball extended far beyond the diamond. In the Dominican Republic and throughout Latino communities, Sosa became a hero. He showed that with hard work and determination, anyone could achieve greatness. Young players in Latin America looked up to him as a role model, inspired by his success and dedication. Sosa's presence in Major League Baseball helped increase the sport's popularity among Hispanic fans. He became a cultural ambassador, bridging gaps and bringing people together through the love of the game. His charisma and passion for baseball resonated with fans, making him one of the most beloved figures in the sport. Sosa's influence in promoting baseball in Hispanic communities is significant. It encouraged more young players to pursue their dreams and aspire to greatness.

However, Sosa's career, as well, was not without its controversies. Allegations of steroid use emerged, casting a shadow over his achievements. These claims, along with his name appearing on a leaked list of players who tested positive in 2003, affected his reputation and legacy. Another blow to his image came in 2003 during a game when his bat shattered, revealing it was corked. Using a corked bat is illegal, as it gives the hitter an unfair advantage by making the bat lighter and easier to swing. This incident led to a suspension, further complicating Sosa's legacy. Despite these challenges, his accomplishments on the field remain part of baseball lore.

Sosa's legacy in the game is complex. His ability to engage fans and hit home runs with unmatched power made him a legend. His story continues to inspire young players, especially in the Dominican Republic, where he remains a symbol of hope and success. Yet, the controversies surrounding his career have sparked ongoing debates about his place in the Baseball Hall of Fame. Sosa has not yet been inducted, with opinions divided on whether his achievements should be recognized despite the allegations. This debate highlights the challenges of balancing a player's on-field success with questions about their integrity. Sosa's influence on baseball and his contributions to fan engagement are undeniable. They have left an indelible mark on the sport, showing that talent and controversy can coexist in the world of baseball.

As we conclude this chapter on home run heroes, we see the power and complexity of the game. Each player brought something unique, shaping baseball's legacy. From towering home runs to the challenges faced, these stories remind us of the sport's enduring appeal. Now, let's move forward to explore the field generals who have commanded the infield with skill and strategy.

CHAPTER 6

FIELD GENERALS

Harmony often starts with the field generals, the infielders who command the diamond. These players are crucial to their team's success. They show leadership and skill, making plays that can decide the outcome of a game. One such player, Cal

Ripken Jr., was known for his incredible durability and impact on the field. His story is one of dedication and inspiration, showing what it means to be a true field general.

6.1 CAL RIPKEN JR.: THE STREAK CONTINUES

Cal Ripken Jr. earned the nickname "Iron Man" for a reason. On September 6, 1995, he broke Lou Gehrig's record by playing in his 2,131st consecutive game. Fans at Camden Yards cheered as the numbers on the scoreboard changed to mark this historic moment. His streak eventually reached 2,632 games, a testament to his commitment and resilience. Cal's dedication to playing every day inspired not just his team, the Baltimore Orioles, but also fans everywhere. In a time when baseball needed a hero, after the 1994 player's strike, Ripken's consistency provided a positive narrative and lifted the spirits of baseball lovers.

Ripken was more than just a durable player. His versatility and skill as an infielder made him a key piece of the Orioles' success. He started his career as a shortstop, a position that demands quick reflexes and agility. As time passed, Cal transitioned to third base, showing his adaptability on the field. His defensive techniques were sharp, allowing him to make plays that seemed impossible. His ability to read the game and anticipate plays was unmatched. This leadership on the field set the standard for infielders and made him a role model for aspiring players. Ripken's influence extended beyond his team, inspiring young athletes to value consistency and dedication.

Offensively, Ripken was a powerhouse. He reached over 3,000 hits in his career, a milestone that only a few players achieve. His batting skills earned him two American League MVP awards and multiple All-Star selections. Cal's impact on the Orioles was immense, contributing to their success with both his bat and his glove. His career achievements made him one of the most respected players in baseball history. Fans admired not just his talent, but also his work ethic and humility. He played the game with passion, always striving to improve and help his team win.

Ripken's legacy is one of perseverance and reliability. He demonstrated that showing up every day, ready to give your best, is a powerful example of commitment. His work ethic inspired countless players, both in baseball and other sports. He showed that true success comes from consistency and dedication. Ripken's emphasis on these values left a lasting mark on the culture of sports, influencing how athletes approach their careers. Young players looked up to him, seeing a player who valued hard work and integrity above all else.

Cal Ripken Jr.'s story is a reminder of the power of dedication and consistency. His achievements on the field are matched by his influence off it, inspiring generations to value hard work and perseverance. He remains a symbol of what it means to be a true field general in the game of baseball.

Reflection Section: The Power of Commitment

Think about a time when you had to show commitment to something important. It could be in sports, school, or another area of your life. How did staying dedicated help you achieve your goals? Reflect on how Cal Ripken Jr.'s story of perseverance might inspire you to keep striving, even when challenges arise.

6.2 OZZIE SMITH: THE WIZARD OF OZ

Ozzie Smith, known affectionately as "The Wizard of Oz," dazzled fans with his exceptional defensive skills. His agility and flair on the field turned routine plays into spectacles of athleticism.

Imagine a shortstop so graceful that he could backflip onto the field, setting the tone for the game before a single pitch was thrown. Smith's acrobatics were more than just showmanship; they were a testament to his incredible athleticism. His ability to make diving catches and lightning-fast throws earned him a remarkable 13 Gold Glove awards. These awards celebrate the best defensive players in the league, and Smith's collection is a testament to his unparalleled skills. He wasn't just a defender; he was a magician on the diamond.

Smith's impact on the shortstop position was profound. Before him, the role focused mainly on basic fielding and throwing. But Smith redefined what it meant to be a shortstop with his quick reflexes and innovative techniques. He made plays that seemed impossible, often leaving fans and teammates alike in awe. His approach to fielding was strategic and methodical. Smith's techniques involved positioning himself perfectly, anticipating where the ball would go, and reacting swiftly. His influence on future generations of shortstops was immense, inspiring many to emulate his style. Players today strive to match his level of play, showcasing the lasting legacy of his innovations.

Throughout his career, Ozzie Smith delivered countless memorable moments. His contributions to the St. Louis Cardinals were significant, helping secure numerous victories with his exceptional fielding. One of the most iconic moments in Smith's career came during the 1985 National League Championship Series. Facing the Los Angeles Dodgers, Smith hit a game-winning home run, which was unexpected from a player known more for his defense than his power. This hit, known as "the shot heard 'round the world," propelled the Cardinals to the World Series and cemented Smith's status as a clutch performer. His ability to shine in crucial moments was a hallmark of his career, making him a beloved figure among St. Louis fans.

Beyond his playing days, Smith has remained an influential figure in baseball. His induction into the Baseball Hall of Fame was a well-deserved honor, recognizing his contributions to the sport. Even after retiring, Smith continues to engage with the baseball community. He shares his love for the game through public appearances and speaking engagements, often advocating for youth involvement in sports. Smith believes in the power of baseball to teach valuable life lessons. He actively encourages young athletes to pursue their dreams and develop their skills. His work with youth programs highlights his commitment to giving back to the community and fostering the next generation of baseball talent.

Ozzie Smith's story is one of talent, innovation, and inspiration. His defensive prowess and charismatic personality made him a standout player. He changed the shortstop position and left a mark on the game that continues to inspire players and fans alike. As a player, he was unmatched in his skill and dedication. As an ambassador for the sport, he remains a guiding light for aspiring athletes. Smith's influence extends far beyond the field, touching the lives of many who look to him as a role model and hero.

6.3 BROOKS ROBINSON: THE HUMAN VACUUM CLEANER

Brooks Robinson didn't just play third base; he transformed it. Many people called him "The Human Vacuum Cleaner" because of his incredible ability to field almost anything that came his way. His skills at third base were legendary. He made plays that seemed impossible, snatching grounders and line drives with ease. Robinson's defensive prowess earned him a record 16 Gold Glove awards. These awards recognized him as the best defensive third baseman in the league year after year. Watching him play was like watching a master at work. He had a knack for making the difficult look routine, and his presence on the field was a comfort to pitchers who knew they could trust him to handle any play.

One of the most memorable moments in Robinson's career came during the 1970 World Series. The Baltimore Orioles faced the Cincinnati Reds, and Robinson's performance was nothing short of spectacular. He made play after play, diving and throwing with pinpoint accuracy. His signature plays in that series helped the Orioles secure victory. Fans still talk about his incredible defense, which was a game-changer. Robinson's impact on the perception of third base was profound. Before him, the position often focused on hitting. But he showed that defensive excellence could be just as valuable. His emphasis on defense set a new standard for third basemen. Other players began to focus more on their fielding skills, inspired by Robinson's success. His influence helped evolve the role of the third baseman, making it a key part of any team's defensive strategy.

Robinson's career was filled with achievements that showcased his talents. He won the American League MVP award and made multiple All-Star appearances. These accolades reflected not only his skill but also his consistency and leadership over two decades. Robinson's ability to perform at a high level year after year was a testament to his dedication and love for the game. He became a fixture in Baltimore, where fans adored him for both his talent and his humility. Robinson's leadership extended beyond the field. He was known for his positive attitude and willingness to support his teammates. His presence in the clubhouse was steady and encouraging. Young players looked up to him, learning from his example and striving to match his commitment.

Off the field, Robinson was just as impressive. He dedicated much of his time to community service and charitable work. In Baltimore, he became a beloved figure, not only for his baseball skills but for his kindness and generosity. He participated in numerous initiatives, giving back to the community that had supported him throughout his career. Robinson's involvement in these efforts showed his dedication to making a difference beyond baseball. His legacy as a player is matched by his impact as a humanitarian. Fans remember him not just as a great third baseman, but as a great person who cared deeply about helping others.

Robinson's influence continues to be felt today, both in Baltimore and the broader baseball community. His story is one of talent, character, and a commitment to excellence. As you reflect on the players who have shaped the game, Brooks Robinson stands out as a true field general, leading with skill and heart. His contributions to baseball and his community have left a lasting mark, inspiring future generations to follow in his footsteps.

6.4 ROBERTO ALOMAR: EXCELLENCE AT SECOND BASE

Roberto Alomar was a standout player who turned second base into an art form. His defensive skills were unmatched, earning him multiple Gold Glove awards. Each award recognized his ability to cover ground quickly, make precise throws, and execute double plays with lightning speed. Alomar's agility allowed him to reach balls that seemed out of reach, making difficult plays look easy. His quick hands and feet helped him turn double plays with efficiency. These skills made him a cornerstone of any defensive lineup. Watching Alomar play second base was like watching a dancer perform. He moved with grace and purpose, always in the right place at the right time. His field awareness and anticipation were key elements of his game, allowing him to coordinate with teammates seamlessly. Alomar's defensive excellence set a high standard for second basemen across the league.

But Alomar was more than just a defensive wizard. He was a true dual-threat player with his offensive skills. His high batting average and on-base percentage showed that he was a force at the plate as well. Alomar had the ability to get on base and drive in runs, making him a valuable asset in any lineup. His bat was as reliable as his glove, and he delivered in clutch situations. During key postseason games, Alomar's hitting played a crucial role in his team's success. His ability to perform under pressure made him a go-to player in tight situations. He had a knack for stepping up when it mattered most, whether it was with a crucial hit or by drawing a walk to spark a rally. Alomar's offensive contributions added another layer to his already impressive skill set, making him one of the most complete players of his era.

Alomar's presence on the field redefined what it meant to be a second baseman. Before him, second basemen were often seen as more defensively oriented, but Alomar changed that perception. He integrated speed and athleticism into the role, showing that second basemen could be dynamic players who impacted both sides of the game. His ability to cover ground and make plays from any angle expanded the expectations for the position. Future generations of second basemen looked to Alomar as a model of excellence, inspired by his style of play. Young players aspired to emulate his combination of speed, agility, and skill. Alomar's influence helped shape a new era of second basemen who could contribute in all aspects of the game.

Beyond his on-field achievements, Alomar's impact on baseball extended to his cultural significance. As a Latino player, he was a trailblazer who opened doors for others to follow. His success helped increase diversity in Major League Baseball, inspiring young Latino players to pursue their dreams. Alomar's induction into the Hall of Fame was a testament to his status as a pioneering figure in the sport. He became a symbol of what could be achieved with talent and hard work, regardless of background. His achieve-ments helped break down barriers and promote inclusivity in the game. Alomar's legacy is one of excellence and inspiration, leaving a lasting impact on the game and its players.

As we move forward, we delve into the next chapter, exploring the pitchers who command the mound and the heart of the game.

CHAPTER 7

FLY CHASERS AND FENCE BUSTERS

7.1 WILLIE MAYS: THE SAY HEY KID

You're at a baseball game, the sky a perfect blue, and the crowd buzzing with anticipation. Suddenly, a crack echoes through the stadium as a ball rockets towards the outfield. In an instant, a player sprints full speed, eyes locked on the ball. With a leap, he makes the catch look effortless, saving the game. This player is Willie Mays, known as "The Say Hey Kid." His prowess in the outfield set a standard few have reached. Mays's defensive skills were nothing short of extraordinary. He had a knack for being in the right place at the right time. His ability to read the ball off the bat was unparalleled. One of his most famous moments, "The Catch," happened during Game 1 of the 1954 World Series source. Mays chased down a deep fly ball hit by Vic Wertz of the Cleveland Indians. At the Polo Grounds, with its deep center field, Mays ran back and made an over-the-shoulder catch at full speed. This play not only saved the game but also became one of the greatest defensive plays in history.

Mays possessed a powerful arm, capable of delivering strong and accurate throws to home plate. His outfield assists were legendary, turning potential runs into outs. Runners thought twice before challenging his arm. His ability to prevent extra bases made him a constant threat to opposing teams. Mays's defensive abilities were complemented by his offensive achievements. Over his career, he hit 660 home runs. This placed him among the all-time greats in power hitting. But he wasn't just about home runs. Mays could hit for average, making him a versatile player. His skills at the plate earned him multiple MVP awards. He consistently performed at a high level, contributing to his team's success. His combination of power and precision made him a force to be reckoned with.

Mays's influence extended beyond his on-field performance. His charisma and style made him a fan favorite. He earned the nickname "The Say Hey Kid" for his friendly demeanor and approachability. Fans connected with him, drawn by his genuine love for the game. Mays became a cultural icon, representing not just baseball but the spirit of determination and joy. His role in the integration of baseball was significant. As an African American player during a time of social change, Mays faced challenges with grace. He became a symbol of hope and progress. His success paved the way for future generations of players, showing that talent knows no color.

Mays's legacy continues to inspire young athletes. His induction into the Baseball Hall of Fame was a testament to his impact on the sport. Aspiring outfielders look up to him as a role model, striving to emulate his skills and dedication. Mays showed what was possible with hard work and passion. His influence reaches far beyond his playing days. He remains a beacon of excellence and a reminder of the joy baseball brings to those who play and watch.

Reflection Section: Willie Mays's Influence

Think about what made Willie Mays such a remarkable player. How did his skills and character impact the game and those who followed him? Reflect on how you can apply lessons from his story to your own life, whether in sports, school, or personal challenges. Consider what it means to lead by example and inspire others through your actions.

7.2 KEN GRIFFEY JR.: GRACE AND POWER

When you think about Ken Griffey Jr., the first thing that might come to mind is his beautiful swing. Griffey's left-handed swing was smooth and powerful, like poetry in motion. It was a swing that kids everywhere tried to copy. Griffey had a natural talent for hitting home runs. Over his career, he hit 630 of them, placing him among the greatest power hitters. But it wasn't just the number of home runs that made him special. It was the way he hit them. Each swing seemed effortless, yet it sent the ball soaring over the fences. This distinctive style made him a standout player, admired by fans and fellow players alike. Griffey's success in the Home Run Derby, where he won back-to-back titles, showcased his incredible power and flair for the dramatic. These victories added to his legend, cementing his place as one of the game's top sluggers.

Griffey wasn't just an offensive powerhouse. His skills in the outfield were equally impressive. As a center fielder, he had a remarkable range, allowing him to chase down fly balls that seemed out of reach. His agility and quick reflexes made him a defensive asset to his team. He won multiple Gold Glove awards, which recognize the best defensive players in the league. Griffey's ability to make difficult catches look routine was a testament to his athleticism and dedication. Watching him patrol the outfield was a treat for fans. He combined speed and grace, moving like a dancer across the grass. His defensive excellence complemented his offensive prowess, making him a complete player who could impact the game in every way.

Off the field, Griffey became a cultural icon. His charisma and charm made him a beloved figure. He was known as "The Kid," a nickname that captured his youthful energy and love for the game. Griffey's popularity soared as he became a marketing phenomenon. He appeared in video games, commercials, and even had his own line of shoes. His appeal extended beyond baseball, reaching fans who might not have followed the sport otherwise. Griffey's influence on a generation of young fans was significant. Kids everywhere wanted to be like him, swinging for the fences and making spectacular catches. His impact on baseball's popularity cannot be overstated. He brought joy and excitement to the game, drawing in new fans and keeping them engaged.

Griffey's contributions to baseball did not end with his playing career. He was inducted into the Hall of Fame with near-unanimous support, a testament to his impact on the sport. His legacy as one of the greatest players of all time is secure. After retiring, Griffey became an ambassador for the sport, promoting baseball and inspiring young athletes. He used his platform to give back to the community, sharing his love for the game with the next generation. Griffey's influence continues to be felt today. Players and fans alike look up to him as a role model and a symbol of what baseball can be. His story is one of talent, passion, and a lasting love for the game.

7.3 MICKEY MANTLE: THE MICK'S LEGACY

Mickey Mantle, known as "The Mick," stood out for his incredible power and unique ability to switch-hit. This means he could bat both left-handed and right-handed, adapting to different pitchers with ease. Mantle's strength was legendary, and he hit over 500 home runs in his career. In 1956, he won the Triple Crown, leading the league in batting average, home runs, and runs batted in. His home runs weren't just numerous; they were majestic. Mantle hit some of the longest home runs ever recorded, with balls traveling incredible distances. His exit velocities, or the speed of the ball off the bat, set records and amazed fans. People came to the ballpark just to see him hit, knowing they might witness something extraordinary. This power, combined with his skill, made Mantle one of the most feared hitters in baseball history.

Despite his impressive achievements, Mantle's career wasn't without its challenges. He faced numerous injuries throughout his time on the field. These included knee problems and other ailments that would have sidelined most players. But Mantle had a remarkable ability to play through pain. His resilience was a testament to his dedication and love for the game. Even when injured, Mantle remained a top performer, contributing to his team's success. His grit and determination inspired his teammates and fans alike. Mantle's perseverance showed that true greatness often comes from pushing through adversity. His ability to overcome setbacks and continue to excel left a lasting impact on those who watched him play. It taught a valuable lesson about the importance of dedication and hard work.

Mantle played a crucial role in the New York Yankees' dynasty during the 1950s and 60s. His presence on the team was a key factor in their success, helping them win seven World Series championships. Mantle's leadership on and off the field brought the team together, creating a strong sense of chemistry. His ability to deliver in clutch moments made him a reliable and trusted figure in the lineup. Teammates looked up to him, and his influence helped shape the team's winning culture. Mantle's contributions to the Yankees went beyond statistics; his leadership and spirit were integral to their dominance in that era. The Mick's impact on the team was profound, cementing his legacy as one of the greatest Yankees of all time.

Culturally, Mantle became a symbol of 1950s and 60s baseball. His charisma and talent made him an American icon. Mantle's popularity transcended the sport, and he appeared in advertisements, movies, and television shows. His image was everywhere, representing the golden age of baseball. Fans adored him for his talent and personality. Mantle's life story captured the imagination of the public, and his influence extended into popular culture. People saw him as more than just a baseball player; he was a hero and a larger-than-life figure. Despite his struggles, Mantle's legacy endured, and his impact on the sport remains significant. His story is a reminder of the power of perseverance and the magic of baseball.

7.4 MIKE TROUT: THE MODERN MARVEL

He hits well, runs fast, fields with skill, throws with power, and can hit the ball out of the park. This is Mike Trout. Many consider him a modern marvel of baseball. Trout's all-around talent makes him a standout player in today's game. He has won multiple MVP awards and has been an All-Star many times. His high batting average and on-base percentage show how consistent he is at the plate. Every season, he impresses with his ability to get on base and score runs. Trout combines power and patience, making him a threat whenever he steps up to hit.

Trout's talents extend beyond hitting. His defensive skills in the outfield are remarkable. Trout is known for making spectacular catches. He covers a lot of ground, thanks to his speed and instincts. Few balls manage to fall for hits when he's on patrol. His ability to track fly balls and make tough plays look easy sets him apart from others. Trout's speed also impacts his base running. He can steal bases and score from almost anywhere on the field. His quickness keeps opponents on their toes, always aware that he might take an extra base. This combination of speed and skill helps his team in many ways. Trout doesn't just play the game; he changes it.

In today's baseball, numbers and data are more important than ever. Trout's performance has helped shape modern baseball analytics. Analysts use advanced metrics to understand what makes him so good. These numbers highlight his value and help teams evaluate players better. Trout's success has influenced how scouts and teams look at talent. Sabermetrics, a method of analyzing baseball through statistics, shows Trout's impact on the game. His consistent performance year after year makes him a benchmark for assessing player skills. Teams now look for players with similar traits: those who can contribute in many areas, just like Trout. He has become a model for what modern players should strive to be.

Young players look up to Trout. They see him as a role model and leader. His work ethic and dedication inspire them to work hard and improve. Trout's influence reaches far beyond the field. He shows young athletes that success comes from hard work and a love for the game. As a mentor, Trout shares his knowledge and passion with others. He supports programs that help young players learn and grow. His positive impact on the next generation of players is clear. Trout has shown that being a great player means more than just having talent. It's about setting a good example and making a positive difference.

Chapter 7 concludes with a look at Trout's incredible skills and impact. His all-around game, from hitting to fielding, sets a high standard. Trout represents what's possible in baseball today. As we move to the next chapter, we'll explore more players who have changed the game and inspired fans.

CHAPTER 8
HAMMERS, FLAMETHROWERS, AND ACES

8.1 NOLAN RYAN: THE STRIKEOUT KING

Nicknamed "The Ryan Express," he became a legend on the mound, leaving a legacy that still inspires pitchers today. Nolan Ryan's career was marked by his incredible ability to overpower hitters. Over his 27 seasons, he set a record with over 5,700 strikeouts, a feat that remains unmatched. Ryan's fastball was his signature weapon, often clocking at speeds that left batters swinging at thin air. He also achieved seven no-hitters, a record that showcased his dominance and skill. Each no-hitter was a testament to his focus and precision, as he faced some of the best hitters in the league and left them without a single hit. These accomplishments made him one of the most feared pitchers in baseball history.

What set Nolan Ryan apart was not just his power but his longevity. He played in Major League Baseball for 27 seasons, an achievement that speaks to his durability and passion for the game. Ryan pitched well into his mid-40s, maintaining a high level of performance. His ability to continue playing at such an advanced age was rare and inspiring. Many pitchers struggle with injuries and fatigue as they age, but Ryan's dedication to his craft kept him at the top of his game. His career spanned four decades and several teams, including the New York Mets, California Angels, Houston Astros, and Texas Rangers. With each team, he brought the same intensity and commitment, earning respect and admiration from fans and fellow players alike.

Ryan's impact on the game extended beyond his playing days. He revolutionized pitching philosophy with his focus on fastball velocity and stamina. He believed in the power of a strong arm and rigorous training. His approach influenced a new generation of pitchers, who sought to emulate his techniques. Ryan was a pioneer in adopting advanced training and conditioning methods, emphasizing the importance of fitness and strength in pitching. His philosophy changed how pitchers prepared for games. He showed that success on the mound required more than talent; it needed dedication and hard work. Ryan's legacy lives on in the way modern pitchers train and compete, proving that his influence on the game is as strong as ever.

After retiring, Ryan continued to shape the sport as a mentor and executive. He took on a leadership role with the Texas Rangers, using his experience to guide young pitchers and influence team development. His presence in the organization brought a wealth of knowledge and insight. Ryan's mentorship helped nurture the next generation of talent, instilling in them the values of hard work and perseverance. His contributions extended beyond strategy and skill, as he also focused on building team morale and fostering a winning culture. Ryan's impact as an executive was as profound as his career on the field, demonstrating his commitment to baseball and his desire to give back to the sport he loved.

Reflection Section: What Makes a Legend?

Think about what makes someone a legend. Is it their achievements, their influence, or their character? Consider how Nolan Ryan's career and legacy can inspire you or the young athletes in your life. Reflect on the qualities that made him a legendary pitcher and how those traits can be applied to your own pursuits.

8.2 SANDY KOUFAX: A LEFTY'S DOMINANCE

Sandy Koufax stands as a beacon of brilliance in baseball history. During his peak years, he achieved feats that many pitchers only dream about. Imagine standing on the mound, facing some of the toughest hitters, and coming out on top time and again. Koufax did just that. He won multiple Cy Young Awards, which recognize the best pitchers in the league. These awards were no small feat, given the fierce competition he faced. In 1963, he also won the National League MVP award, underscoring his incredible influence on the game. But perhaps his most legendary moment came in 1965. Facing the Chicago Cubs, Koufax pitched a perfect game. Not a single batter reached base. It was a performance of sheer precision and control, one that left fans and fellow players in awe. His ability to dominate on the mound was unparalleled, making him one of the greatest left-handed pitchers of all time.

Koufax's success was not just about raw talent. His strategic approach to pitching set him apart. He had a devastating curveball that left batters guessing. With pinpoint accuracy, he could place the ball exactly where he wanted. This precision made him almost untouchable. Koufax knew how to use pitch sequences to confuse hitters. By changing speeds and locations, he kept batters off balance. They never knew what was coming next. His understanding of the game and ability to read opponents made him a master on the mound. His technique and control became the gold standard for pitchers everywhere. Young players looked up to him, hoping to learn from his skills and emulate his success.

Despite his remarkable achievements, Koufax's career came to an unexpected halt. At the height of his powers, he faced a challenge that no amount of skill could overcome. Chronic elbow pain plagued him, making it difficult to continue at the level he demanded of himself. In 1966, at just 30 years old, Koufax made the difficult decision to retire. This choice shocked the baseball world. Many wondered what more he could have achieved had he continued to play. Yet, his early retirement did not diminish his legacy. Instead, it added to his mystique. Fans and players alike marveled at what he accomplished in such a short time. His decision to leave the game while still at his peak only reinforced his status as a legend. He left on his terms, maintaining the high standards he set for himself.

Koufax's influence on baseball continues to this day. In 1972, he was inducted into the Baseball Hall of Fame, becoming the youngest player ever to receive this honor at the time. His induction was a testament to his impact on the game. Koufax represented excellence and integrity, qualities that resonate deeply in the world of sports. He inspired countless pitchers to strive for greatness, using their skills to reach new heights. Beyond his technical brilliance, Koufax became a cultural icon. He symbolized the perfect blend of talent and humility, showing that true greatness lies in both ability and character. His legacy remains a guiding light for those who seek to make their mark on baseball, reminding us all of the power of dedication and passion.

8.3 PEDRO MARTINEZ: CRAFTING MASTERY

Pedro Martinez stands out in baseball history as a pitcher who could control the game with his skill, intelligence, and flair. In the late 1990s and early 2000s, Martinez was a force to be reckoned with. He won the Cy Young Award three times, a testament to his unmatched abilities on the mound. Each season, he led the league in ERA and strikeouts multiple times. This showed how dominant he was in his era. His unique style of pitching kept batters guessing, never knowing what to expect next. Pedro's talent was not just about throwing hard; it was about using his mind as much as his arm.

Martinez's approach to pitching was a masterclass in strategy. He had a vast array of pitches at his disposal and knew exactly how to use each one. He varied his pitch speeds and locations with precision, keeping hitters off balance. This ability to change things up made him unpredictable. Batters couldn't settle into a rhythm against him. Pedro's psychological tactics played a big part in his success. He studied hitters closely, learning their weaknesses, and exploited them with ease. His adaptability on the mound was second to none. If one plan didn't work, he quickly switched to another, always staying one step ahead of his opponents. This mental edge often turned the tide in his favor.

Pedro's impact on the Boston Red Sox was profound. His arrival signaled a new era for the team. His performances were key to breaking the "Curse of the Bambino," a championship drought that had haunted the Red Sox for 86 years. In the 2004 World Series, Martinez delivered when it mattered most. His pitching helped lead the Red Sox to a historic victory, ending the long wait for a title. Beyond his on-field heroics, Pedro's influence in the clubhouse was immense. He brought leadership, confidence, and a winning mindset. Teammates looked up to him, inspired by his work ethic and determination. His presence transformed the team, instilling a belief that they could achieve greatness.

Martinez's legacy extends far beyond his playing days. He became a trailblazer for Latino players, paving the way for many who followed in his footsteps. His success showed that talent could come from anywhere, regardless of background. In 2015, Martinez was inducted into the Baseball Hall of Fame, a fitting recognition of his contributions to the sport. His influence is felt on an international scale. Young players around the world look up to him as a role model, drawn to his story of perseverance and success. Even after retiring, Pedro remains active in baseball. He serves as a mentor to aspiring pitchers, sharing his knowledge and experiences. He also works as a commentator, offering insights that only someone of his caliber can provide.

Pedro Martinez's story is about more than just stats and records. It's about passion, dedication, and the joy of playing baseball at the highest level. His journey from a small town in the Dominican Republic to the pinnacle of the sport inspires everyone who hears it. Pedro's legacy continues to grow, as his influence reaches new generations of fans and players. His name will forever be linked with excellence, creativity, and the love of the game.

8.4 MARIANO RIVERA: THE CLOSER'S ROLE

Mariano Rivera, known as the greatest closer in baseball history, redefined what it meant to finish a game. Imagine a game in the ninth inning, tension high, and the outcome hanging in the balance. Rivera would step onto the mound, and with calm confidence, he would shut down the opposing team. He holds the all-time record for saves, an incredible 652, making him the undisputed leader in this crucial role. Rivera's performances were not just about numbers; they were about moments. In 13 All-Star games and multiple World Series, he showed up every time. His presence on the Yankees was a cornerstone of their dynasty, providing the backbone for some of the team's most memorable victories.

What made Rivera stand out was his signature pitch, the cut fastball. It was simple yet devastating. With a grip that seemed effortless, Rivera could make the ball move sharply at the last moment. Hitters knew it was coming, but they still struggled to make solid contact. This pitch carved through bats and dashed hopes, earning him a reputation as nearly untouchable. Rivera's consistency was legendary. In the toughest situations, he maintained his cool, delivering pitch after pitch with pinpoint accuracy. His ability to remain composed and effective, even with the game on the line, set him apart. Rivera turned high-pressure moments into opportunities to shine, showing that true greatness lies in simplicity and focus.

Rivera's influence on the role of the closer transformed how teams approached the final innings. Traditionally, relief pitchers were seen as secondary to starters. Rivera changed this perception, elevating the closer's role to one of strategic importance. Managers began to rely on their bullpens more, knowing that a strong closer could turn the tides of a game. Rivera's success showed that the back end of the bullpen was just as vital as the start. His approach influenced how teams managed their pitching strategies, emphasizing the need for a reliable finisher. This evolution in the game highlighted Rivera's impact, proving that he wasn't just winning games; he was shaping the future of baseball.

Beyond his achievements on the field, Rivera's legacy extends into the broader baseball community. In 2019, he became the first player ever inducted into the Hall of Fame unanimously, a testament to the respect he earned from peers and fans alike. This honor recognized not only his incredible skill but also his character. Rivera was known for his humility and grace, qualities that endeared him to many. Off the field, he dedicated himself to philanthropy, focusing on helping those in need. His leadership within the Yankees' organization extended beyond the diamond, as he worked to inspire and uplift others. Rivera's contributions to the game and his community cemented his place as a role model, showing that being a great athlete also means being a great person.

Mariano Rivera's career is a testament to the power of skill, dedication, and character. His role as a closer changed the landscape of baseball, proving that the final innings are as vital as the first pitch. As we look to the future, Rivera's influence remains, inspiring new generations to aim high and play with heart. His story is a reminder that true greatness is not just in what you achieve, but in how you achieve it.

CHAPTER 9

HONORING THE PIONEERS

9.1 SATCHEL PAIGE: A TRAILBLAZER IN THE NEGRO LEAGUES

The pitcher stands tall on the mound, his every move watched by eager eyes. The crowd waits, not knowing what trick he might pull next. This was the magic of Satchel Paige, a man whose legend began long before he stepped into the major leagues. His journey started in the Negro Leagues, a parallel world of baseball where talent shined brightly, away from the segregated major leagues. Satchel Paige became a star with the Kansas City Monarchs. His performances drew crowds who marveled at his unique style. He mastered the art of pitching with his signature "Hesitation Pitch," a move that left batters guessing. This pitch was more than a trick. It was a symbol of his creativity and skill, showing that baseball was as much about wits as it was about physical strength.

Paige's journey from the Negro Leagues to the Major Leagues marked a significant shift in baseball history. In 1948, he signed with the Cleveland Indians, becoming one of the first black pitchers in Major League Baseball. His arrival was more than just a personal achievement. It was a step toward breaking down the racial barriers that had long kept talented black players from competing at the highest level. Paige showed that talent and hard work know no color. His success opened doors for others, paving the way for future generations of black athletes to enter the major leagues. His influence on the integration of baseball was profound. He helped change the way the game was played and who got to play it.

Satchel Paige's personality was as big as his talent. Known for his charisma and quick wit, he captivated fans both on and off the field. His famous quotes and stories added to his legend. Once, when asked about his age, Paige famously replied, "How old would you be if you didn't know how old you are?" His words reflected his playful nature and timeless spirit. Paige was more than just a player. He was a showman who knew how to entertain and engage an audience. His presence helped popularize the Negro Leagues, drawing attention to the incredible talent within. Fans from all backgrounds came to see him pitch, and in doing so, they gained a greater appreciation for the skill and passion of Negro League players.

Paige's legacy extends far beyond his playing days. His induction into the Baseball Hall of Fame in 1971 was a recognition of his impact on the game. It was a testament to his skill and the barriers he helped break. Paige's story continues to inspire both African American and non-African American athletes. He showed that with talent and perseverance, anything is possible. His journey is a reminder of the challenges faced by those who paved the way for others. Paige remains a symbol of resilience and talent, a figure who changed the course of baseball history. His influence is felt in every pitch thrown by those who followed in his footsteps.

Reflection Section: The Power of Perseverance

Think about Satchel Paige's journey and the obstacles he overcame. Consider the importance of perseverance in achieving your goals. How can Paige's story inspire you or the young people in your life to push through challenges and strive for success, no matter the odds?

9.2 CONNIE MACK: THE GRAND OLD MAN OF BASEBALL

Imagine a baseball manager who spent over half a century guiding a single team. That was Connie Mack, a true icon of the sport. He managed the Philadelphia Athletics for an astounding 50 years. During this time, he became known for his strategic mind and calm demeanor. Mack's career in baseball was unprecedented. He became a central figure in shaping how the game was played and managed. As a manager, he led his team through many highs and lows. His ability to adapt and innovate kept him at the forefront of baseball for decades. Mack's influence on the sport was far-reaching, laying the groundwork for modern managerial techniques.

Mack had a keen eye for talent, which he used to build strong teams. He focused on scouting and recognizing potential in young players. This approach allowed him to nurture talent and develop future stars. Mack knew that building a championship team required more than just signing big names. He believed in the power of teamwork and chemistry. By carefully selecting players who complemented each other, he created cohesive units that worked well together. His knack for making strategic trades also helped him build winning teams. These trades often brought in key players who made a significant impact. Mack's emphasis on player development and team building set a standard that managers still follow today.

Beyond his role as a manager, Mack was also a savvy businessman. He served as both manager and owner of the Athletics, which gave him unique insights into the financial side of baseball. Mack understood the importance of balancing budgets while building competitive teams. He often faced financial challenges, particularly during tough economic times. Despite these obstacles, he found creative ways to keep his team afloat. Mack's financial strategies and team management skills contributed to the economic growth of baseball. He showed how the sport could thrive as a business while maintaining its integrity. His dual role allowed him to influence both the game and its business aspects.

Mack's legacy in baseball is unmatched, with his record for most wins as a manager standing as a testament to his success. He amassed over 3,700 wins throughout his career, a feat that few have come close to matching. His longevity and impact on the game earned him a well-deserved place in the Baseball Hall of Fame. Mack's contributions to the sport continue to be revered, as he left an indelible mark on baseball history. His innovative approach to managing and team building influenced generations of managers and players. Mack's focus on nurturing talent and creating cohesive teams laid the foundation for future success. His ability to adapt and thrive in a rapidly changing sport ensured his legacy would endure.

Connie Mack's impact on baseball extended beyond his managerial skills. He became a symbol of the game's enduring appeal and the possibilities it offered. His dedication and passion for the sport inspired countless others to pursue careers in baseball. Mack's influence is still felt today, as his principles and strategies continue to guide the sport. His story serves as a reminder of the power of perseverance and innovation in shaping the future. Mack's contributions to baseball were not just about wins and losses. They were about creating a lasting legacy that would inspire future generations. His vision for the game and his commitment to excellence helped shape baseball into the beloved sport it is today.

9.3 CASEY STENGEL: A MANAGERIAL LEGEND

Casey Stengel was a one-of-a-kind manager who brought creativity and flair to baseball. Imagine a man who could take a team and make it more than just a group of players. Stengel did just that with his innovative approach to managing. He believed in using platoon systems, which meant playing different players based on who they were up against. This strategy allowed him to maximize the strengths of his team, ensuring that they had the best chance to win each game. Stengel was not afraid to rotate players, giving everyone a chance to contribute. His methods kept his team fresh and adaptable, ready to face any challenge. This flexible approach made his teams unpredictable and often gave them an edge over their opponents.

Stengel's personality was as colorful as his strategies. He was known for his humor and wit, which endeared him to players and fans alike. His speeches, filled with funny stories and wise sayings, were famous in baseball circles. Stengel's ability to lighten the mood helped keep his team relaxed and focused. He knew that a happy team was a successful one. His jokes and colorful language became part of his charm, making him a beloved figure in the sport. Stengel's unique style of communication helped him connect with players, building strong relationships that were crucial to his success. His ability to blend humor with strategy made him a standout manager.

Under Stengel's leadership, the New York Yankees became a baseball powerhouse. He guided them to 10 American League pennants and seven World Series championships. These achievements solidified his reputation as one of the greatest managers in history. Stengel's success with the Yankees was no accident. He had a keen eye for talent and knew how to bring out the best in his players. His ability to make smart decisions under pressure was key to the team's triumphs. Stengel understood the importance of teamwork and instilled a winning mentality in his players. His leadership created a dynasty that dominated baseball for years.

Stengel's influence went beyond winning games. He had a remarkable talent for managing diverse personalities. On a team, different players bring different strengths, and Stengel knew how to get them to work together. He developed strong team cohesion, ensuring that every player understood their role and contributed to the team's success. Stengel's adaptability allowed him to handle changing player dynamics over time. He understood that each player had unique needs and abilities, and he tailored his approach to fit those needs. This flexibility helped him build teams that were not only talented but also unified and resilient.

Casey Stengel's legacy in baseball is enduring. His induction into the Baseball Hall of Fame recognized his impact on the sport. Stengel's innovative style continues to inspire modern coaches and managers. They look to his methods as a blueprint for building successful teams. His emphasis on flexibility, humor, and strong relationships remains relevant in today's game. Stengel's influence can be seen in how teams are managed, with many adopting his strategies to great effect. His story is a reminder of the power of creativity and connection in achieving greatness in baseball.

9.4 BRANCH RICKEY: THE ARCHITECT OF CHANGE

Branch Rickey saw baseball not just as a game but as a stage for change. His vision for baseball stretched far beyond the diamond. He was a pioneer who introduced the farm system for developing talent. This transformed how teams nurtured their players. Instead of relying solely on established stars, teams could now cultivate young talent. Rickey set up minor league teams where players could hone their skills. This system allowed them to grow and improve before stepping onto the major league stage. It was like building a strong foundation for a house. Rickey's farm system gave baseball a steady stream of skilled players ready to shine.

Rickey's contributions didn't stop with player development. He made one of the most significant moves in baseball history by signing Jackie Robinson. This decision broke the color barrier. It was a bold step that changed the sport forever. In 1947, Robinson became the first African American to play in Major League Baseball. This was a time when racial segregation was common. Rickey saw beyond the barriers and focused on talent and character. His decision to bring Robinson into the league was more than just a baseball move. It was a statement about equality and justice. Rickey believed in giving everyone a fair chance, regardless of their background. This move paved the way for future generations of diverse players to enter the sport.

Rickey's strategic vision extended to how he managed teams. He understood the importance of developing not just skills but also character. He emphasized education for his players, ensuring they were well-rounded individuals. Rickey believed that a good player was also a good person. This focus on character helped build strong teams with players who respected the game and each other. Rickey's approach to management was innovative. He looked at the big picture and planned for the future. By developing the minor league system, he created a pipeline of talent that benefited not just his teams but the entire league. His methods showed that success wasn't just about winning games. It was about building a solid foundation for sustained excellence.

Rickey's influence went beyond baseball. He was an advocate for civil rights and social justice. His actions helped promote integration and diversity, not just in sports but in society. Rickey's decision to sign Robinson was a powerful message against segregation. It showed that baseball could lead the way in breaking down racial barriers. His advocacy for equality and fairness made a lasting impact on Major League Baseball's commitment to diversity. Rickey's leadership helped shape a more inclusive sport. It encouraged others to follow his example and stand up for what is right. His work in promoting social change showed that baseball could be a force for good, inspiring positive change both on and off the field.

Branch Rickey's legacy is profound. His induction into the Baseball Hall of Fame recognizes his contributions to the sport. He remains a visionary leader whose ideas continue to influence baseball. Rickey's impact is seen in the ongoing recognition of his innovations. The farm system he created is still in use today, providing a steady flow of talent to the major leagues. His commitment to diversity and equality set a standard that the league continues to uphold. Rickey's vision and leadership helped shape baseball into the sport we know today. His influence is felt in every corner of the game, from player development to team management and beyond. His legacy serves as a reminder of the power of vision and courage in driving meaningful change.

CHAPTER 10
RISING STARS OF THE GAME

10.1 FERNANDO TATÍS JR.: THE NEW FACE OF BASEBALL

When Fernando Tatís Jr. steps onto the field, he immediately changes the game. Born into a baseball family, Tatís grew up with the game in his blood. His father,

Fernando Tatís Sr., also played in the majors, setting the stage for his son's career. Tatís Jr. made his MLB debut with the San Diego Padres in 2019, and since then, he has become one of the most exciting players to watch. His style of play is dynamic and versatile. He can hit with power and run with speed. This makes him a threat both at the plate and on the bases.

Tatís Jr. uses his powerful bat to drive the ball deep into the outfield. He often hits home runs that leave fans in awe and his speed allows him to steal bases and score runs. But his talents don't stop there. As a shortstop, he performs acrobatic plays that turn potential hits into outs. He dives, jumps, and throws with precision, showcasing his athleticism and quick reflexes. These plays not only excite fans but also save runs for his team. His defensive skills are a big part of what makes him such a valuable player.

Beyond his skills on the field, Tatís Jr. connects with younger audiences. He represents a new generation of baseball players who bring energy and excitement to the sport. He uses social media to engage with fans, sharing highlights and personal moments. This interaction helps grow the game's popularity among young people. By connecting with fans in this way, Tatís makes baseball more relatable and fun. His presence helps the sport reach new audiences, keeping it fresh and exciting.

Tatís Jr.'s charisma and marketability set him apart from many other players. His appeal crosses cultural boundaries, making him a global ambassador for baseball. Companies see his potential and often partner with him for endorsements and brand deals. These partnerships extend his influence beyond the baseball diamond, reaching fans around the world. Tatís's ability to connect with people from different backgrounds shows his universal appeal. This makes him a role model for aspiring athletes everywhere.

Looking forward, Tatís Jr.'s future in baseball shines bright. He has the potential to achieve significant milestones and break records. His pursuit of MVP titles and other accolades is just beginning. With his talent and determination, he could set new standards in batting and base stealing. His career trajectory suggests that he will continue to be a dominant force in the league. Fans eagerly watch his progress, anticipating the many achievements that lie ahead.

Reflection Section: The New Face of Baseball

Consider how players like Fernando Tatís Jr. influence young fans. Reflect on how his style and personality make the game appealing. Think about what this means for the future of baseball and how you can support young athletes in your life.

10.2 JUAN SOTO: A YOUNG PHENOM

When you watch Juan Soto step into the batter's box, you see a player wise beyond his years. His approach at the plate is something that even seasoned veterans admire. Soto has a keen eye for the strike zone, which is why he often draws walks. His patience is remarkable, allowing him to wait for the perfect pitch. This results in a high on-base percentage, making him a constant threat to any pitcher. His power-hitting abilities are just as impressive. Soto can send the ball soaring into the stands with ease, leaving fans cheering for more. It's rare to see such a blend of power and discipline in a young player, but Soto makes it look effortless.

Soto's rise in Major League Baseball has been nothing short of meteoric. In 2019, he played a crucial role in the Washington Nationals' World Series win. His performances in the postseason were key to their success. Soto showed that he could handle pressure, delivering when it mattered most. Achieving milestones like 100 career home runs at such a young age only adds to his growing list of achievements. These accomplishments aren't just numbers; they speak to his talent and determination. Soto's rapid rise shows how quickly he has become one of baseball's brightest stars.

Within the Washington Nationals, Soto is more than just a great player. He is a leader who inspires those around him. His presence in the lineup rejuvenates the team, bringing energy and excitement. Younger players look up to him, learning from his focus and work ethic. Soto's influence extends to the clubhouse, where he fosters a positive environment. His leadership qualities help build team dynamics, making the Nationals a cohesive unit. Through his actions and attitude, Soto shows that leadership is about more than words—it's about setting an example.

Soto's impact goes beyond the field, reaching into the hearts of fans around the world. In the Dominican Republic, where he was born, young players see him as a hero. He inspires them to dream big and believe in their potential. Soto's success shines a light on the talent that comes from Latin America. His participation in international events and collaborations strengthens his role as an ambassador for the sport. He bridges cultures, uniting fans through their love for baseball. Soto's influence helps grow the game globally, making it more inclusive and exciting for everyone.

10.3 RONALD ACUÑA JR.: SPEED AND POWER

Ronald Acuña Jr. is a player who captures attention the moment he steps onto the field. His combination of speed and power makes him stand out in Major League Baseball. When Acuña picks up a bat, you can sense the excitement in the air. He swings with force, sending balls soaring over the fence. His ability to hit home runs with ease is matched by his remarkable speed. Acuña races around the bases like a lightning bolt, stealing bases and scoring runs. His quick starts and aggressive base running keep opponents on their toes. They never know when he might take off, turning a simple hit into an opportunity for more.

Acuña's contributions to the Atlanta Braves are undeniable. He plays a key role in their success, helping the team secure playoff spots and division titles. In high-pressure situations, Acuña shines. He delivers clutch performances when the stakes are high, proving his worth time and again. His presence in the lineup boosts the Braves' chances of winning. Teams know that with Acuña on the field, anything can happen. His energy and skills inspire his teammates to give their best. Acuña not only elevates his own game but also raises the level of those around him. His impact on the Braves is clear, making him a vital part of their achievements.

Acuña's potential for achieving historic feats is immense. He has set his sights on reaching the coveted 40-40 mark, a rare achievement in baseball. This means hitting 40 home runs and stealing 40 bases in a single season. If anyone can do it, Acuña can. His ability to combine power and speed puts him in a league of his own. He also aims to break franchise records and set new benchmarks for future players. With every game, he gets closer to these goals, leaving fans excited about what he might achieve next. Acuña's career continues to rise, and his potential seems limitless.

Beyond his skills, Acuña brings entertainment to the game. His charismatic celebrations and interactions with fans make baseball more exciting. Whether it's a joyous dance after a home run or a playful gesture to the crowd, Acuña knows how to engage his audience. His flair for showmanship increases attendance and viewership. Fans flock to see him play, knowing they're in for a treat. Acuña's ability to entertain goes hand in hand with his talent, making him a favorite among fans of all ages. His presence on the field turns a regular game into an event, filled with moments that keep everyone on the edge of their seats.

10.4 VLADIMIR GUERRERO JR.: CARRYING THE LEGACY

Vladimir Guerrero Jr. comes from a family where baseball is more than just a game. It's a legacy. His father, Vladimir Guerrero Sr., is a Hall of Famer known for his incredible skills and powerful arm. Growing up, Guerrero Jr. watched his father play, learning from him both the art of the game and the dedication it takes to succeed. These early lessons shaped Guerrero Jr.'s own aspirations. Baseball was in his blood, and he wanted to follow in his father's footsteps. With a bat in his hand, he dreamed of making his own mark on the game. His family ties are a constant source of inspiration, driving him to reach new heights and honor the Guerrero name.

Guerrero Jr.'s power-hitting abilities have made him a standout player. When he steps up to the plate, he brings a presence that commands attention. His swings are strong and precise, often leading the league in home runs and RBIs. Just one swing from Guerrero Jr. can change the outcome of a game. This power makes him a key player in any lineup, capable of turning the tides with a single hit. His offensive prowess is not just about raw strength; it's about timing and technique. Guerrero Jr. knows how to read a pitch and adjust his swing to connect perfectly. Each time he hits a home run, it serves as a reminder of his talent and potential.

As Guerrero Jr. continues to grow as a player, he shows remarkable adaptation to the challenges of Major League Baseball. Facing skilled pitchers requires constant improvement, and Guerrero Jr. has risen to the occasion. His plate discipline has improved, allowing him to wait for the right pitch and make better contact. This patience has enhanced his hitting, making him even more dangerous at the plate. His defense has also seen development, as he adapts to different roles and responsibilities on the field. Whether playing first base or covering ground in the outfield, Guerrero Jr. demonstrates versatility and commitment to his craft. These improvements highlight his dedication to becoming a well-rounded player.

Looking ahead, Guerrero Jr.'s potential for future accolades is immense. He strives for MVP awards and batting titles, goals that are well within his reach. His career trajectory suggests that he could even surpass his father's achievements, a prospect that excites fans and analysts alike. With each season, Guerrero Jr. adds to his legacy, setting new records and leaving his mark on the game. His path is one of ambition and hard work, fueled by his desire to excel and honor the Guerrero name. As he continues to evolve, the baseball world watches with anticipation, eager to see what he will accomplish next. His journey is a testament to the power of family, talent, and perseverance in shaping the future of baseball.

In Chapter 11, we'll explore the fierce rivalries and unforgettable matchups that have defined Major League Baseball. These stories bring to light the passion and competition that make the sport so captivating.

CHAPTER 11
MLB MATCHUPS AND RIVALRIES

11.1 YANKEES VS. RED SOX: A RIVALRY FOR THE AGES

The New York Yankees and the Boston Red Sox have battled on the field for over a century, crafting a narrative filled with drama and passion. This rivalry is not just about baseball. It's a tale woven into the very fabric of American sports culture. The roots of this fierce competition go back to 1919. That year, Red Sox owner Harry Frazee sold Babe Ruth to the Yankees, an event that changed baseball history. Ruth, a pitcher-turned-slugger, transformed the Yankees into a powerhouse. His sale marked the beginning of what many called the "Curse of the Bambino," a supposed jinx that kept the Red Sox from winning the World Series for 86 long years. This narrative added a layer of mystique to every game between these teams.

The rivalry reached a fever pitch in the 2004 American League Championship Series. The Yankees had a commanding 3-0 lead, and it seemed like the Red Sox would fall once again. But something incredible happened. The Red Sox fought back, winning four straight games to take the series. This comeback was historic. No team had ever overcome such a deficit in baseball's postseason. This victory not only ended the supposed curse but also set the stage for the Red Sox to win the World Series that year. The 2004 ALCS remains one of the most iconic moments in sports, showcasing the rivalry's intensity and the unpredictable nature of baseball.

Beyond the games, the Yankees and Red Sox rivalry has left a mark on the culture of New York and Boston. These cities have long been rivals in more than just sports. They compete in economics and culture, fueling the fire between their baseball teams. The rivalry is a reflection of this broader competition. When these teams meet, it's not just a game. It's an event that captures the attention of fans across the nation. These matchups are among the most-watched MLB games, bringing people together in shared anticipation and excitement. The rivalry also influences local economies, boosting tourism as fans travel to support their teams. The games become a celebration of regional pride, with each city eager to claim victory over the other.

Throughout history, the Yankees and Red Sox have produced unforgettable moments and legendary players. One such moment came in 1978 when Bucky Dent hit a home run that shattered Boston's hopes in a one-game playoff. Known as the "Boston Massacre," this game remains etched in the memories of fans. The fierce pitching duels between Pedro Martinez and Roger Clemens added another layer of excitement. These battles showcased the skills and determination of two of baseball's best pitchers. Such moments define the rivalry, highlighting the blend of talent and tension that makes each game a spectacle.

As time passes, the dynamics of the Yankees and Red Sox rivalry continue to evolve. Recent postseason matchups have kept the rivalry alive, with each team striving to outdo the other. Player trades and free agency have also added new twists. Players sometimes switch sides, bringing their talents and insights to their former rivals. These changes keep the rivalry fresh, as new players step into the spotlight, eager to make their mark. The intensity remains, fueled by history, competition, and the desire to be the best.

Reflection Section: Your Favorite Rivalry Moment

Think about a memorable Yankees vs. Red Sox game you've watched or heard about. What made it special to you? Was it a dramatic play, a favorite player, or the atmosphere of the rivalry? Reflect on how these moments connect fans, creating shared experiences and lasting memories.

11.2 CARDINALS VS. CUBS: MIDWEST SHOWDOWNS

St. Louis and Chicago, separated by a few hundred miles, have long been home to one of baseball's fiercest rivalries. This rivalry isn't just about baseball. It's about regional pride. These two cities boast rich histories and distinct cultures. The proximity of St. Louis and Chicago adds fuel to the fire, making every matchup between the Cardinals and Cubs more than just a game. It's a chance for each city to prove its worth and claim bragging rights in the Midwest. When these teams meet, fans from both sides feel the tension and excitement. They know that this isn't just another game.

Throughout the years, this rivalry has seen its share of unforgettable moments and legendary players. One of the most memorable times was during the summer of 1998. Mark McGwire of the Cardinals and Sammy Sosa of the Cubs captivated the nation with their home run race. Both players were chasing history, trying to break the single-season home run record. Every time they stepped up to the plate, fans held their breath. It was a thrilling showdown that kept everyone on the edge of their seats. This race wasn't just about individual glory. It became a symbol of the rivalry itself, showcasing the power and passion of both teams. Another significant figure in this rivalry is Stan Musial. Musial, a Cardinals legend, made a habit of dominating the Cubs whenever they faced off. His prowess on the field added to the intensity of the competition. Every hit and home run he made against the Cubs was a reminder of St. Louis's strength.

Fans play a crucial role in keeping this rivalry alive and vibrant. Each year, Wrigley Field and Busch Stadium become battlegrounds for these teams and their supporters. These series are eagerly anticipated events. Fans from both cities travel to cheer on their team, turning the stadiums into seas of red or blue. This tradition of road trips and away games adds another layer of excitement. It's not just about watching the game. It's about being part of the experience, sharing in the highs and lows with fellow fans. The chants, cheers, and jeers create an atmosphere that's electric and charged with emotion. For many, attending these games is a rite of passage, a way to connect with their community and share in a long-standing tradition.

The rivalry between the Cardinals and Cubs also impacts how both teams approach the game. Managers and players understand the importance of these matchups. They know that a win against their rival can change the course of a season. As a result, teams often make strategic roster changes and moves during these games. They want to put their best foot forward and give their fans a reason to celebrate. Rivalry games can also influence playoff races and outcomes. A victory over a rival not only boosts morale but can also shift momentum in a team's favor. This added pressure and intensity push players to perform at their highest level, showcasing the very best of baseball.

The Cardinals and Cubs rivalry remains a testament to the enduring appeal of baseball. It's a story of passion, pride, and competition that continues to captivate fans year after year. As new players take the field and fans fill the stands, the legacy of this rivalry only grows stronger.

11.3 GIANTS VS. DODGERS: COAST-TO-COAST COMPETITION

When you think of baseball rivalries, the Giants and Dodgers come to mind. These teams began their fierce competition back in New York. The Giants called the Polo Grounds home, while the Dodgers played at Ebbets Field in Brooklyn. Fans packed the stands every time these two teams faced off. It was more than just a game. It was a battle for pride and bragging rights. The rivalry took a dramatic turn in 1951 with the "Shot Heard 'Round the World." Bobby Thomson of the Giants hit a spectacular home run to clinch the pennant, sending the Polo Grounds into a frenzy. That moment became a defining point in the history of the rivalry.

In the late 1950s, both teams made a bold move to the West Coast. The Dodgers settled in Los Angeles, and the Giants made San Francisco their new home. This shift brought the rivalry to California, creating a new competitive landscape. Baseball fans on the West Coast quickly embraced the rivalry. The games between the Giants and Dodgers became must-see events, drawing huge crowds. The move helped build a strong and loyal fan base for both teams. Fans from all over California came to support their teams, creating a vibrant baseball culture. This rivalry helped solidify baseball's presence on the West Coast, making it a key part of the region's sports identity.

Throughout the years, many players have left their mark on this rivalry. Jackie Robinson, who broke baseball's color barrier, played a crucial role in the early years. His presence on the Dodgers added intensity to the rivalry. He faced off against some of the Giants' best, showcasing his talent and determination. Then there's the infamous brawl between Juan Marichal of the Giants and John Roseboro of the Dodgers. This clash in 1965 was a heated moment that highlighted the fierce competition between the teams. It reminded everyone that this rivalry was not just about skill but also about passion and pride. These moments are etched in the memories of fans, adding to the lore of the Giants-Dodgers rivalry.

In recent years, the rivalry has continued to thrive. The teams have faced each other in intense postseason matchups and division battles. These games are filled with drama and excitement, as both teams fight for dominance. New players have emerged, eager to make their names in the rivalry's history. Management strategies have evolved, with teams using data and analytics to gain an edge. Trades and acquisitions have brought fresh talent to the field, adding new dynamics to the competition. The rivalry remains a highlight of the MLB season, capturing the hearts of fans across the country.

11.4 METS VS. PHILLIES: A BATTLE OF THE EAST

When you think about baseball on the East Coast, the rivalry between the New York Mets and the Philadelphia Phillies stands out. This rivalry didn't just appear overnight. It grew during the late 20th century, fueled by intense divisional battles. In the 1980s, both teams found themselves fighting for the top spot in their division. The stakes were high, and every game felt like a playoff. The rivalry truly heated up in the 2007 and 2008 seasons. During these years, the Phillies overtook the Mets in dramatic fashion, clinching division titles that left Mets fans heartbroken. These games added layers of tension and excitement, making the rivalry even more intense.

The close proximity of New York and Philadelphia plays a big role in this rivalry. Just a short train ride separates these two cities. Fans can easily travel to attend games, bringing their energy and passion with them. This geographical closeness adds to the rivalry's intensity. It's not uncommon for fans of both teams to fill the opposing stadiums, creating a charged atmosphere. The media also plays its part in amplifying the rivalry's narrative. Local newspapers and sports channels cover every matchup, often highlighting past grudges and memorable moments. This coverage keeps fans engaged and makes each game feel like a must-see event.

Many players have left their mark on the Mets-Phillies rivalry. Mike Piazza, a Mets icon, often faced off against the Phillies' pitching staff. His powerful hitting and presence at the plate made him a key figure in many games. Piazza's battles with Phillies pitchers were thrilling, showcasing his talent and determination. On the Phillies side,

Jimmy Rollins emerged as a leader and pivotal player. His leadership and clutch performances helped guide the Phillies during crucial games. Rollins' ability to deliver in high-pressure situations made him a fan favorite and a constant thorn in the Mets' side. These players and their contributions are etched in the memories of fans, making each game between the teams a part of baseball history.

Today, the Mets-Phillies rivalry continues to evolve. Recent seasons have seen both teams battling for playoff spots, adding more drama to their encounters. Divisional races are often tight, with each game carrying significant weight. Player trades and free agency have also shifted the dynamics. New faces bring fresh energy and rivalries, while familiar ones add depth to the story. The rivalry remains a highlight of the baseball season, drawing attention and excitement from fans. As both teams strive for success, they carry with them the history and passion that define this rivalry.

As we close this chapter, it's clear that these rivalries are more than just games. They are stories of passion, pride, and competition. Each rivalry has its unique flavor, bringing excitement and history to the sport. These matchups remind us why baseball holds a special place in our hearts. In the next chapter, we'll explore the great teams and moments that have made baseball the beloved game it is today.

CHAPTER 12
GREAT MLB TEAMS AND MOMENTS

12.1 THE 1927 YANKEES: MURDERERS' ROW

Y ou've stepped into a time machine and traveled back to the roaring 1920s. The world is full of jazz, flapper dresses, and the crack of a baseball bat echoing through the stands. In this vibrant era, the 1927 New York Yankees stood tall and proud, a team that would become legendary in the annals of baseball history. Known as "Murderers' Row," this team was a powerhouse, a lineup of hitters so formidable that opposing pitchers trembled at the thought of facing them.

The 1927 Yankees boasted a lineup that was the envy of the baseball world. At the heart of this team were two of the game's greatest hitters: Babe Ruth and Lou Gehrig. Ruth, often called "The Sultan of Swat," was not just a player. He was an icon. His towering home runs captivated fans and set new standards in power hitting, with 60 home runs that season. Next to him, Lou Gehrig, known as "The Iron Horse," was just as formidable. Gehrig had a batting average of .373, a testament to his skill and consistency. Together, they formed a duo that was unmatched in baseball history. But the Yankees were not just about Ruth and Gehrig. Earle Combs and Tony Lazzeri added depth to this already impressive lineup. Combs, with his speed and keen eye, was a master at getting on base, setting the stage for the big hitters. Lazzeri, known for his clutch hitting, provided the extra punch that made the Yankees' offense unstoppable. Their combined efforts created a lineup that could score runs at will, earning the nickname "Murderers' Row."

The Yankees' success was not just about talent. It was about strategy and leadership. Manager Miller Huggins was a master tactician. He knew how to get the best out of his players. Huggins emphasized a balance between power and precision, ensuring that every player knew their role and played to their strengths. His leadership style was calm and composed, instilling confidence in his team. This approach allowed the Yankees to maintain a level of consistency that few teams could match. The team's batting strategy focused on power and accuracy. They had the ability to hit home runs, but they also excelled at getting on base and moving runners along. This combination made them nearly unbeatable. Opposing teams struggled to keep up with the Yankees' relentless offense. The 1927 season became a showcase of their dominance, with the Yankees setting records and leaving their mark on baseball history.

The cultural and historical impact of the 1927 Yankees cannot be overstated. They changed the way people viewed baseball, setting a new standard for excellence. The concept of "Murderers' Row" became synonymous with greatness, a benchmark for future teams to aspire to. This team showed that baseball could be both thrilling and strategic, a game of skill and power. The Yankees' success inspired generations of young players, each dreaming of emulating their heroes. The legacy of the 1927 Yankees continues to influence baseball today, reminding us of the heights that can be achieved through talent, teamwork, and determination.

The Yankees' 1927 season was one for the record books. They finished with an astounding 110 wins, a testament to their dominance and skill. This impressive record set them apart as one of the best teams in baseball history. But their success didn't end with the regular season. In the World Series, the Yankees faced the Pittsburgh Pirates. They swept the series, winning four games in a row. This victory cemented their status as champions, a team that could rise to any occasion. The Yankees' performance in 1927 was more than just a string of victories. It was a statement of their prowess, a declaration of their place in baseball history. The season remains a shining example of what a team can achieve when talent and strategy come together in perfect harmony.

Reflection Section: What Made the 1927 Yankees Great?

Reflect on what you think made the 1927 Yankees so successful. Was it their powerful hitters, their strategy, or something else? Consider how a team working together towards a common goal can achieve greatness.

12.2 THE SHOT HEARD 'ROUND THE WORLD: BOBBY THOMSON'S LEGENDARY HOMER

The year is 1951. The New York Giants found themselves in a tense battle, one that baseball fans still talk about today. On August 11, the Giants were 13 games behind their fierce rivals, the Brooklyn Dodgers. The season seemed lost, but the Giants had other plans. They mounted an incredible comeback, winning 39 of their last 47 games. This comeback set the stage for a dramatic three-game playoff series, a thrilling showdown to decide who would claim the National League pennant.

As the final game of the series began, the atmosphere was electric. The Polo Grounds in New York buzzed with anticipation. Fans filled every seat, eager to witness history in the making. The Dodgers took an early lead, but the Giants fought back, refusing to give in. By the ninth inning, the tension was almost unbearable. The Dodgers had a slight edge, leading 4-2. It seemed like they might hold on for the win. Then came the moment that would forever be etched in the memory of baseball fans.

Bobby Thomson, a player known for his clutch performances, stepped up to the plate. Ralph Branca, the Dodgers' pitcher, prepared to face him. The crowd held its breath. With one swing, Thomson changed everything. He connected with Branca's pitch, sending it soaring into the left-field stands. The ball disappeared over the fence, and pandemonium erupted. The Giants had done it. They won the game 5-4. Russ Hodges, the Giants' radio announcer, captured the moment perfectly. His voice filled with emotion, he shouted, "The Giants win the pennant! The Giants win the pennant!" Those words, carried over the airwaves, became as legendary as the homer itself.

Thomson's home run was more than just a game-winner. It became a symbol of triumph and drama, a defining moment in baseball's rich history. The excitement and shock of that instant resonated far beyond the Polo Grounds. It showed the world what baseball could be: unpredictable, thrilling, and full of heart. The home run helped solidify baseball's place in American culture, demonstrating the sport's ability to captivate the nation. Fans across the country were glued to their radios, sharing in the joy and disbelief of the Giants' victory.

The impact of Thomson's homer reached far beyond that October day. It inspired future generations of players and fans alike. Young kids dreaming of the big leagues imagined themselves in Thomson's shoes, hitting that game-winning shot. It taught fans that in baseball, as in life, anything is possible. The moment became a beacon of hope, reminding people that even when the odds seem insurmountable, perseverance can lead to victory. The story of the "Shot Heard 'Round the World" continues to be told, passed down through families, each retelling capturing the magic of that day.

Today, the legacy of Bobby Thomson's home run lives on. It remains one of the most cherished parts of baseball lore. Each year, fans and historians look back, commemorating the moment with documentaries, books, and even reenactments. The story of the 1951 pennant race and Thomson's homer has been depicted in movies and discussed in countless articles. It serves as a reminder of the power of sports to unite and inspire. The rivalry between the Giants and Dodgers endures, fueled by the history they share, with Thomson's homer standing as a testament to their fierce competition.

Thomson's home run is more than a memory. It is an enduring symbol of what makes baseball special. The drama, the excitement, and the spirit of competition all come together in that single swing. As fans continue to celebrate and remember the "Shot Heard 'Round the World," they keep alive the essence of baseball. The sport's ability to create unforgettable moments, to bring people together, and to inspire dreams remains as strong as ever.

12.3 JACKIE ROBINSON'S DEBUT: CHANGING THE GAME FOREVER

On April 15, 1947, a young man named Jackie Robinson stepped onto the field for the Brooklyn Dodgers, forever changing the landscape of Major League Baseball. This day marked the end of racial segregation in the sport, as Robinson became the first African American to play in the major leagues in the modern era. His debut was more than just a game. It was a powerful statement against the long-standing racial barriers that had kept black players out of the big leagues. Robinson's presence on the field signaled a new beginning, one that promised change and progress. Fans packed the stands, witnessing history unfold before their very eyes. Robinson's performance that day was solid, showcasing his skill and determination. He hit a crucial single, stole a base, and his quick reflexes on the field helped the Dodgers secure a victory. Yet, the significance of his debut went beyond statistics. It was about courage, resilience, and the start of a movement that would ripple across the nation.

The road to Robinson's debut was fraught with challenges. Throughout his first season, Robinson faced hostility from many angles. Some fans jeered and hurled racial slurs, while certain players refused to take the field with him. Despite this, Robinson remained steadfast. He focused on his game, proving his worth through talent and hard work. The pressure he faced was immense, yet he never faltered. His ability to remain composed in the face of adversity was nothing short of remarkable. Robinson's teammates played a crucial role in his journey, offering support and solidarity. Pee Wee Reese, a fellow Dodger, famously stood by Robinson, placing his arm around him during a particularly tense game. This simple act of friendship spoke volumes, showing that some were willing to stand against discrimination and support change. It highlighted the power of allyship and the importance of unity in the fight for equality.

Robinson's debut transcended sports, becoming a pivotal moment in the broader struggle for civil rights. His presence in Major League Baseball was a beacon of hope, signaling that change was possible. Robinson became a symbol of equality and perseverance, inspiring countless others to challenge the status quo. His courage on the field mirrored the courage of those fighting for civil rights across the country. Robinson's impact extended beyond baseball, influencing the civil rights movement and encouraging others to push for social justice. He showed that sports could be a platform for change, a powerful tool for challenging injustice and promoting equality. Robinson's actions inspired a generation of activists, athletes, and ordinary people to stand up for what was right.

The legacy of Jackie Robinson's breakthrough continues to shape baseball and society today. Each year, Major League Baseball celebrates Jackie Robinson Day on April 15, honoring his achievements and the path he paved for future generations. On this day, players across the league wear his iconic number, 42, keeping his memory alive and highlighting his enduring influence. Robinson's legacy extends beyond commemorations. His story has inspired ongoing initiatives aimed at promoting diversity and inclusion in sports. Programs and scholarships in his name continue to support young athletes from diverse backgrounds, ensuring that everyone has the opportunity to succeed. Robinson's life and career serve as a reminder of the power of sports to drive change and inspire hope.

Robinson's impact on baseball and society is profound and lasting. He showed the world that talent knows no color and that perseverance can overcome even the most entrenched barriers. His legacy serves as a beacon of hope and inspiration, encouraging us to continue striving for equality and justice. Robinson's story reminds us of the importance of courage, unity, and the relentless pursuit of a fairer world. His contributions to baseball and society are a testament to the power of determination and the enduring impact of one person's bravery. As we reflect on Robinson's achievements, we are reminded of the ongoing journey toward equality and the role each of us can play in making the world a better place.

Jackie Robinson's debut was a moment that changed the game forever, leaving an indelible mark on baseball and society. His courage and determination paved the way for future generations, inspiring countless others to follow in his footsteps. As we look to the future, Robinson's legacy continues to inspire us to strive for a more inclusive and equitable world, both on and off the field. His story is a powerful reminder of the enduring impact of one person's bravery and the transformative power of sports.

CHAPTER 13
INSPIRATIONAL MLB
TALES

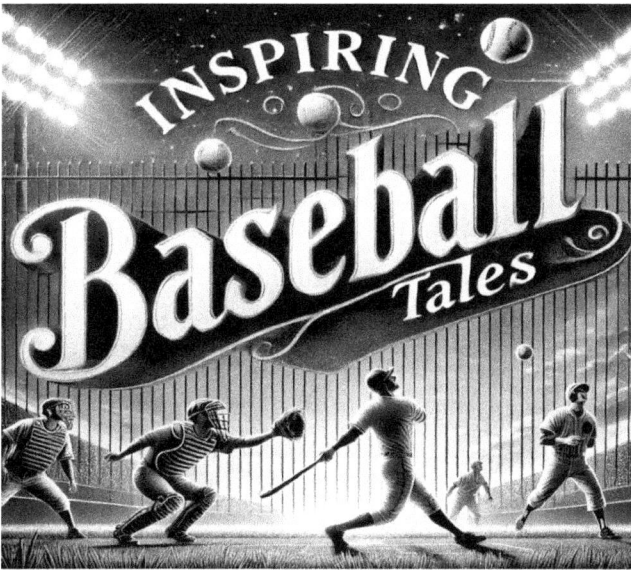

13.1 LOU GEHRIG'S FAREWELL: THE LUCKIEST MAN SPEECH

Picture a packed Yankee Stadium on a warm July 4th. The stands buzz with anticipation, not for a game, but for a moment that would etch itself into the hearts of all present. Lou

Gehrig, the beloved "Iron Horse," stood poised to address the crowd. His career had been a testament to endurance and excellence, marked by 2,130 consecutive games played. Yet, this day was different. Gehrig faced a new challenge—amyotrophic lateral sclerosis, known as ALS, a disease that had cut his career short. It was on this day that Gehrig would deliver a speech that still resonates, known as the "Luckiest Man" speech.

As Gehrig stepped up to the microphone, there was a solemn hush. Instead of focusing on his illness, Gehrig expressed deep gratitude. He thanked his teammates, fans, and family for their unwavering support. His words were simple yet powerful, capturing the essence of humility. "Today, I consider myself the luckiest man on the face of the Earth," he declared. This line, delivered with sincerity, moved everyone. Gehrig's grace and resilience in the face of adversity left a lasting impression on all who heard him that day. His ability to focus on blessings rather than misfortune was a lesson in dignity and strength.

Gehrig's farewell speech did more than touch those in attendance. It rippled across the baseball community and beyond. His courage in addressing his condition brought attention to ALS, a disease largely unknown at the time. In the years following his speech, awareness grew, leading to initiatives aimed at finding a cure. Gehrig's example set a standard for sportsmanship and character. His willingness to face his challenges head-on inspired others to do the same. Athletes and fans alike found motivation in his words, seeing him as a beacon of hope in difficult times.

Today, Gehrig's legacy continues to inspire. Annual ALS awareness events in Major League Baseball honor his memory, keeping the fight against the disease in the public eye. His speech remains a cultural touchstone, referenced in media and literature for its timeless message of gratitude and resilience. These tributes ensure that Gehrig's spirit lives on, reminding us of the power of humility and courage in overcoming life's challenges. His story is a testament to the enduring impact of one man's words and character.

Reflection Section: Gratitude in Adversity

Think about a time when you faced a challenge. How did you find strength and hope? What can we learn from Gehrig's ability to remain grateful despite adversity? Share these thoughts with someone close to you, and reflect on the power of gratitude in your own life.

13.2 JIM ABBOTT: TRIUMPH OVER PHYSICAL CHALLENGES

Imagine a boy who loves baseball more than anything. He dreams of stepping onto the mound in a major league stadium, and he doesn't let anything stop him. This was Jim Abbott, born without a right hand, yet determined to play the game he loved. Growing up, Abbott faced many challenges. People doubted his ability to play baseball at a high level. But Abbott didn't see his condition as a barrier. Instead, he saw it as a chance to prove what he could do. He worked tirelessly to improve his skills, developing a unique way to pitch and field that set him apart from others.

Abbott's dedication paid off. He made it to the major leagues, achieving what many thought impossible. One of his most memorable moments came on September 4, 1993, when he pitched a no-hitter for the New York Yankees against the Cleveland Indians. A no-hitter is a rare and difficult feat. It requires a pitcher to hold the opposing team hitless for an entire game. This achievement was even more remarkable given the challenges Abbott faced. Just five days before, the same team had hit him hard. Abbott's ability to rise above and deliver an outstanding performance showed his true strength and determination.

Abbott's success wasn't just about his physical skills. It was also about his mindset. He focused on what he could do, not what he couldn't. Abbott developed special techniques to handle the ball, switching his glove to and from his hand with ease. His adaptability on the field inspired many. He showed that with creativity and hard work, obstacles could be overcome. Abbott's career in the major leagues was a testament to his perseverance. His story reminds us all that determination can lead to success, no matter the challenges we face.

Beyond his achievements on the field, Abbott became a role model for athletes with disabilities. He changed how people saw ability in sports. Abbott advocated for inclusive sports programs, encouraging others to pursue their dreams regardless of physical limitations. His story has inspired many young athletes who face similar challenges. He taught them that they too could reach their goals with determination and hard work. Abbott's influence extended beyond baseball. He became a motivational speaker, sharing his story with audiences around the world. His message of resilience and hope inspired countless people to overcome their challenges.

Abbott's dedication to helping others didn't stop there. He supported charitable organizations focused on disability awareness. His efforts helped raise awareness and support for those with physical challenges. Abbott's story continues to motivate and inspire. His life shows that with effort and belief in oneself, anything is possible. His journey from a boy with a dream to a major league pitcher is a powerful reminder that our limitations do not define us. It's our determination and courage that truly make us who we are.

<u>Reflection Section: Overcoming Challenges</u>

Think about a challenge you have faced. How did you overcome it? What can you learn from Jim Abbott's determination and adaptability? Share your thoughts with someone you trust and reflect on how you can apply these lessons to your own life.

13.3 ROBERTO CLEMENTE: A LIFE OF SERVICE AND SACRIFICE

Roberto Clemente was more than just a baseball player. He was a hero both on and off the field. Standing in the batter's box, he wielded his bat with precision and power, amassing over 3,000 hits in his career. His skill in the outfield was unmatched, earning him numerous Gold Glove awards. Fans admired his graceful movements as he chased down fly balls and made impossible throws look easy. Clemente's passion for the game was evident in every play, but his heart extended far beyond the diamond. He dedicated himself to helping others, especially those in his native Puerto Rico and other Latin American countries. He believed in using his platform for good and made a lasting impact through his humanitarian work.

Clemente was a fierce advocate for social justice and equality. He knew firsthand the challenges faced by Latino players in Major League Baseball. Using his voice, he pushed for better treatment and opportunities for these players. He was not afraid to speak out against discrimination and worked tirelessly to promote fairness and respect in the sport. Clemente's commitment to civil rights extended beyond baseball. He championed causes that uplifted underrepresented communities and fought for social equality. He wanted everyone to have a fair chance and used his influence to make the world a better place.

Tragedy struck on December 31, 1972, when Clemente died in a plane crash. He was on a mission to deliver aid to earthquake victims in Nicaragua. This selfless act was a testament to his character. His untimely death shocked the baseball world and beyond. It highlighted the risks he took to help others, even at the cost of his own life. Clemente's passing left a void, but his legacy of service and sacrifice inspired many. His commitment to community service became a guiding light for Major League Baseball, encouraging players to engage in philanthropic efforts.

Clemente's legacy lives on through various honors and recognitions. The Roberto Clemente Award remains one of the most prestigious in baseball. It goes to players who excel on the field and demonstrate outstanding community involvement. This award keeps Clemente's spirit alive, encouraging players to follow his example. In Puerto Rico and across the baseball community, celebrations and tributes honor his contributions. Schools, parks, and foundations bear his name, serving as reminders of his impact. His story teaches us the importance of using our talents to help others and the power of giving back. Clemente's life of service continues to inspire, reminding us that true greatness lies in what we do for those in need.

13.4 JACKIE ROBINSON: BEYOND BASEBALL

Jackie Robinson's impact on the world didn't end when he hung up his baseball cleats. Instead, his influence grew as he stepped into a new role as a leader in the fight for civil rights. After breaking barriers as the first African American in Major League Baseball, Robinson used his fame to speak out against racial injustice. He saw the world beyond the diamond, and he wanted to make it better for everyone. He became a powerful voice in the Civil Rights Movement, working alongside other leaders to advocate for equality and justice. His efforts went beyond mere words; they were actions that helped shape a new era.

Robinson established the Jackie Robinson Foundation, which has made a lasting impact by supporting education for young people. He believed education was key to unlocking opportunities for African Americans. By providing scholarships and mentoring, the foundation helped countless students achieve their dreams. Robinson knew that education could change lives, and he wanted to ensure that young people had the chance to succeed. This foundation stands as a testament to his belief in the power of education and opportunity. His work in this area has opened doors for many, creating a legacy that continues to grow.

Robinson's role as a leader didn't stop with education. He actively participated in political and social initiatives, pushing for change in all areas of life. He spoke out against discrimination and worked to create economic opportunities for African Americans. Robinson understood the importance of leveling the playing field in all aspects of society. He advocated for equal job opportunities and fair housing, using his platform to highlight these critical issues. His commitment to these causes was unwavering, and his voice carried weight in the halls of power. By challenging the status quo, he inspired others to join the fight for justice.

His influence extends far beyond his lifetime, inspiring future generations of athletes and activists. Robinson served as a mentor and role model, showing what was possible with determination and courage. His legacy lives on in the many athletes who see him as a symbol of perseverance and dedication. Robinson's life and work have influenced the intersection of sports and social activism, demonstrating how athletes can use their platforms for positive change. He paved the way for others to follow, leaving a trail of inspiration that continues to guide those who seek to make a difference.

The celebration of Robinson's contributions continues today. Every year, Major League Baseball honors his legacy with Jackie Robinson Day. On this day, players across the league wear his iconic number 42, a tribute to his impact on the game and society. This tradition serves as a reminder of Robinson's courage and the progress he helped foster. Educational programs and initiatives inspired by his life keep his memory alive, teaching new generations about his contributions. Robinson's story is more than a chapter in history; it's a living legacy that continues to inspire and guide.

As we close this chapter, we see how Robinson's life transcended the game. He showed us the power of courage and conviction in the face of adversity. His legacy is a beacon of hope and determination, inspiring us to strive for a better world. Now, as we move forward, we look to the future, where the lessons of the past guide us toward new possibilities.

LOVE THE BOOK?
HERE'S HOW YOU CAN HELP!

If you or your child enjoy *A Kid's Guide to Baseball Legends,* we'd love to hear your thoughts! Leaving a review on Amazon is a great way to support me and share your feedback with others. By leaving a review, you're helping other young readers discover this fantastic book.

How to Leave a ★★★★★ Review on Amazon

1. **Go to the Amazon page** for *A Kid's Guide to Baseball Legends.*
2. Scroll down to the "Customer Reviews" section.
3. Click on the "Write a Customer Review" button.
4. Share what you loved about the book – Was it the inspiring stories? The legendary players?
5. Hit "Submit" – And that's it!

Don't Wait – Share Your Thoughts Today!

CONCLUSION

Throughout this book, we have embarked on a journey to uncover the magic of baseball. The goal has always been to inspire you and the young readers in your life. Baseball is not just a game. It is a treasure trove of stories, history, and lessons. Through our chapters, we aimed to ignite a passion for this rich sport. We wanted to connect you with the legends of the past and the icons of today. Our hope is that this book helps you see baseball as more than just a sport. It is a bridge to understanding teamwork, perseverance, and resilience.

We began by exploring the birth of Major League Baseball. We saw how early games evolved into the beloved sport we know today. We learned about the notable figures who shaped the game. We delved into the inspiring stories of legends like Babe Ruth and Jackie Robinson. These figures not only changed the game but also impacted society in profound ways. We discovered the modern-day icons who continue to inspire, like Derek Jeter and Ichiro Suzuki. Their stories remind us of the dedication and love required to excel. We also highlighted unforgettable moments and rivalries that have defined baseball history. Each chapter aimed to bring to life the vibrant world of baseball. We wanted you to feel the excitement of a home run and the tension of a fierce rivalry.

The key takeaways from this book are simple yet powerful. Baseball teaches us important life lessons. Teamwork helps us achieve more together than alone. Perseverance shows us the value of never giving up, even when things get tough. Resilience is about bouncing back from setbacks and staying strong. The characters and stories in this book serve as role models. They guide us on how to overcome obstacles and achieve greatness. These lessons extend beyond the field. They are tools you can use in everyday life.

Now, I invite you to reflect on your own experiences with baseball or any sport. Think about the lessons you have learned and the memories you cherish. Use the stories from this book as a starting point for discussions with children. Share the joy and history of baseball with them. This can help foster a deeper appreciation for the game. It can also spark meaningful conversations about values and life lessons.

I encourage you to take action. Share this book and its stories with others. Attend a baseball game with your family. Explore baseball history further through books or documentaries. Participate in local baseball activities. By doing so, you help continue the tradition and love for the sport. You also inspire the next generation to embrace the values that baseball teaches.

I want to express my heartfelt gratitude to you for joining me on this journey. I hope the stories and insights in this book have sparked a passion for baseball in you and your young readers. May these tales inspire them to dream big and pursue their passions. Remember the dedication and spirit shown by the legends of the game. Let it guide you and the children in your life toward your own dreams.

To close, I leave you with a quote from Jackie Robinson: "A life is not important except in the impact it has on other lives." Let this reminder of Robinson's legacy inspire you to make a positive impact. As you carry forward the lessons learned, may you find joy and purpose in every step of your journey.

REFERENCES

History Cooperative. (n.d.). *Origins of baseball: Evolved out of cricket and rounders.* https://historycooperative.org/origins-of-baseball/

Baseball Reference. (n.d.). *Knickerbocker rules - BR bullpen.* https://www.baseball-reference.com/bullpen/Knickerbocker_Rules

History.com Editors. (n.d.). *Cincinnati Red Stockings become first professional baseball team.* https://www.history.com/this-day-in-history/first-professional-baseball-team-cincinnati-red-stockings

Travel World Magazine. (2022, June). *Legendary ballparks: Fenway and Wrigley.* https://www.travelworldmagazine.com/2022/06/legendary-ballparks-fenway-and-wrigley/#:.

Major League Baseball. (n.d.). *From ace to yakker, a glossary of baseball slang.* https://www.mlb.com/news/best-baseball-slang-terms

National Baseball Hall of Fame. (n.d.). *A history of the baseball uniform - Introduction.* http://exhibits.baseballhalloffame.org/dressed_to_the_nines/introduction.htm

Baseball Monkey. (n.d.). *Baseball equipment list: Essential baseball gear checklist.* https://www.baseballmonkey.com/learn/youth-baseball-equipment-guide

Baseball Monkey. (n.d.). *150+ common baseball words, slang & jargon.* https://www.baseballmonkey.com/learn/baseball-terms-slang-defined

National Baseball Hall of Fame. (n.d.). *The Babe's called shot.* https://baseballhall.org/discover-more/stories/baseball-history/called-shot

Prospect. (n.d.). *Jackie Robinson: A legacy of activism.* https://prospect.org/civil-rights/jackie-robinson-legacy-activism/

National Baseball Hall of Fame. (n.d.). *Luckiest man: Lou Gehrig's farewell speech.* https://baseballhall.org/discover-more/stories/baseball-history/lou-gehrig-luckiest-man

Wikipedia. (n.d.). *T206 Honus Wagner.* https://en.wikipedia.org/wiki/T206_Honus_Wagner

Wikipedia. (n.d.). *Derek Jeter.* https://en.wikipedia.org/wiki/Derek_Jeter

Cressey, E. (n.d.). *What Albert Pujols taught me about swing mechanics.* https://ericcressey.com/albert-pujols-swing-mechanics/

The Ringer. (2021, September 14). *The colossal legacy of Ichiro's rookie season, 20 years later.* https://www.theringer.com/mlb/2021/9/14/22664414/ichiro-suzuki-seattle-mariners-2001-rookie-season-legacy

Wikipedia. (n.d.). *Clayton Kershaw.* https://en.wikipedia.org/wiki/Clayton_Ker shaw#:

National Baseball Hall of Fame. (n.d.). *Henry Aaron hits home run No. 715.* https:// baseballhall.org/discover-more/stories/inside-pitch/henry-aaron-hits-home-run-number-715

Historic Baseball. (n.d.). *Barry Bonds - Controversy and unmatched slugging in baseball.* https://historicbaseball.com/barry-bonds-controversy-and-unmatched-slug ging-in-baseball/

Wikipedia. (n.d.). *1998 Major League Baseball home run record chase.* https://en.wiki pedia.org/wiki/1998_Major_League_Baseball_home_run_record_chase

Society for American Baseball Research. (n.d.). *Sammy Sosa.* https://sabr.org/ bioproj/person/sammy-sosa/

National Baseball Hall of Fame. (n.d.). *Cal Ripken breaks Lou Gehrig's record.* https:// baseballhall.org/discover/inside-pitch/cal-ripken-breaks-lou-gehrigs-consecu tive-games-record

Wikipedia. (n.d.). *Ozzie Smith.* https://en.wikipedia.org/wiki/Ozzie_Smith

Major League Baseball. (n.d.). *Top 10 moments of Brooks Robinson's career.* https:// www.mlb.com/news/brooks-robinson-best-career-moments

Major League Baseball. (n.d.). *Latino players in Baseball Hall of Fame.* https://www. mlb.com/news/latino-players-in-baseball-hall-of-fame

Wikipedia. (n.d.). *The catch (baseball).* https://en.wikipedia.org/wiki/The_ Catch_(baseball)

Bleacher Report. (n.d.). *How '90s icon Ken Griffey Jr. transcended MLB to become a pop culture legend.* https://bleacherreport.com/articles/2896652-how-90s-icon-ken-griffey-jr-transcended-mlb-to-become-a-pop-culture-legend

Wikipedia. (n.d.). *Mickey Mantle.* https://en.wikipedia.org/wiki/Mickey_Mantle

Baseball Savant. (n.d.). *Mike Trout stats: Statcast, visuals & advanced metrics.* https:// baseballsavant.mlb.com/savant-player/mike-trout-545361

National Baseball Hall of Fame. (n.d.). *Nolan Ryan.* https://baseballhall.org/hall-of-famers/ryan-nolan

Wikipedia. (n.d.). *Sandy Koufax.* https://en.wikipedia.org/wiki/Sandy_Koufax#:.

1918 Red Sox. (n.d.). *Pedro Martinez's impact on the Boston Red Sox.* https://1918red sox.com/blog/pedro-martinez-red-sox-legend.htm#:.

Pinstripe Alley. (2019, January 23). *How Mariano Rivera rode one pitch all the way to the Hall.* https://www.pinstripealley.com/2019/1/23/18193746/yankees-mari ano-rivera-baseball-hall-of-fame-unanimous-selection-cutter-cut-fastball

Major League Baseball. (n.d.). *Satchel Paige.* https://www.mlb.com/history/negro-leagues/players/satchel-paige

Society for American Baseball Research. (n.d.). *Connie Mack: The tall tactician.* https://sabr.org/journal/article/connie-mack-the-tall-tactician/

Wikipedia. (n.d.). *Casey Stengel*. https://en.wikipedia.org/wiki/Casey_Stengel#:

Library of Congress. (n.d.). *Breaking the color line: 1940 to 1946*. https://www.loc. gov/collections/jackie-robinson-baseball/articles-and-essays/baseball-the-color-line-and-jackie-robinson/1940-to-1946/

Wikipedia. (n.d.). *Fernando Tatís Jr.*. https://en.wikipedia.org/wiki/Fernando_Tat% C3%ADs_Jr.

Baseball Reference. (n.d.). *Juan Soto stats, height, weight, position, rookie status & more*. https://www.baseball-reference.com/players/s/sotoju01.shtml

Sports Illustrated. (n.d.). *Another historic look at how insane Ronald Acuna Jr.'s 2021 season was*. https://www.si.com/fannation/mlb/fastball/history/atlanta-braves-star-became-first-player-in-more-than-100-years-of-baseball-history-to-lead-league-in-stolen-bases-and-total-bases

Wikipedia. (n.d.). *Vladimir Guerrero Jr.*. https://en.wikipedia.org/wiki/ Vladimir_Guerrero_Jr.#:~

Wikipedia. (n.d.). *Yankees–Red Sox rivalry*. https://en.wikipedia.org/wiki/Yankees% E2%80%93Red_Sox_rivalry

Major League Baseball. (n.d.). *The top six moments in the history of the Cubs-Cardinals rivalry*. https://www.mlb.com/cut4/five-best-moments-in-the-cubs-cardinals-rivalry-c256494120

Major League Baseball. (n.d.). *Dodgers vs. Giants best moments*. https://www.mlb. com/news/dodgers-vs-giants-best-moments

Major League Baseball. (n.d.). *The Mets-Phillies rivalry's best, most notable games*. https://www.mlb.com/news/best-games-in-mets-vs-phillies-history

Wikipedia. (n.d.). *Murderers' row*. https://en.wikipedia.org/wiki/Murderers% 27_Row

Major League Baseball. (n.d.). *Bobby Thomson's shot heard 'round the world*. https:// www.mlb.com/news/bobby-thomson-shot-heard-round-the-world-off-ralph-branca

The Sports Museum. (n.d.). *The great influence of Jackie Robinson*. https://www. sportsmuseum.org/the-great-influence-of-jackie-robinson/

FanArch. (n.d.). *The top 10 greatest teams in MLB history*. https://fanarch.com/blogs/ fan-arch/the-top-10-greatest-teams-in-mlb-history?srsltid=AfmBOorDEhT g9WmHmfeLdiqFbh5WAFdUvOA4Ru4jVYQRAKtOp-NqZGwx

Buckley School. (n.d.). *Lou Gehrig's farewell speech: The luckiest man*. https://www. buckleyschool.com/magazine/articles/lou-gehrigs-farewell-speech-the-lucki est-man/

CNN. (2023, September 4). *The legacy of Jim Abbott and the night of that no-hitter*. https://www.cnn.com/2023/09/04/sport/jim-abbott-legacy-no-hitter-spt-intl/ index.html

Society for American Baseball Research. (n.d.). *Roberto Clemente, humanitarian*.

https://sabr.org/journal/article/roberto-clemente-humanitarian/

Major League Baseball. (n.d.). *Jackie Robinson fought for civil rights off the field.* https://www.mlb.com/news/jackie-robinson-fought-for-civil-rights-off-the-field

AUTHOR BIO

Kent Jameson grew up in a quaint farm town in Iowa, where he developed a deep appreciation for the simplicity of rural life. In 1994, he earned a Bachelor of Science degree in Family and Consumer Sciences Journalism from Iowa State University.

When he's not writing, Kent enjoys spending time with his two sons, often cheering them on from the sidelines as they play basketball. Currently residing in Phoenix, Arizona, he continues to live by the small-town values that have guided him throughout his life and career.

www.ingramcontent.com/pod-product-compliance
Lightning Source LLC
LaVergne TN
LVHW051417080426
835508LV00022B/3123